Shenandoah

Shenandoah

A Story of Conservation and Betrayal

SUE EISENFELD

University of Nebraska Press
Lincoln & London

Acknowledgments for the use of copyrighted
material appear on page 167, which constitutes an
extension of the copyright page.

Library of Congress
Cataloging-in-Publication Data

Eisenfeld, Sue.
Shenandoah: a story of conservation
and betrayal / Sue Eisenfeld.
pages   cm
Includes bibliographical references.
ISBN 978-0-8032-3830-5 (pbk.: alk. paper)
ISBN 978-0-8032-6540-0 (epub)
ISBN 978-0-8032-6541-7 (mobi)
ISBN 978-0-8032-6539-4 (pdf)
1. Shenandoah National Park (Va.)—History—20th
century. 2. Appalachians (People)—Virginia—
Shenandoah National Park—History—20th century.
3. Eminent domain—Virginia—History—20th
century. 4. Carson, William E. (William Edward),
1871–1942. I. Title.
F232.S48E35 2014
975.5'9—dc23
2014023127

Set in Swift EF by Renni Johnson.

For Neil

The journey is an evocation of three things . . . : a landscape that is incomparable, a time that is gone forever, and the human spirit, which endures.

—N. SCOTT MOMADAY, *The Way to Rainy Mountain*

Contents

Author's Note

FOR THOSE OF YOU who are tempted to find all the places I've described in this book, I give this guidance: For your safety, please know that only experienced, well-conditioned hikers, familiar with Shenandoah National Park, the use of map and compass, leave-no-trace philosophy, risk prevention, and wilderness first aid and outfitted with the proper maps, gear, and equipment should even consider off-trail hiking. The National Park Service and Shenandoah's rangers advise hikers to follow only the formal system of blazed trails (near which plenty of history can be found—many of the trails are former roads and are located in areas once inhabited), so that you do not become lost, stranded, or injured or require an expensive and time-consuming rescue. The park also advises hikers to stay on the marked trails to protect park resources, such as rare plants, and to prevent erosion.

Please always behave with respect when examining the signs of human habitation, here and in any other protected area. Not only is the removal or disturbance of natural objects or historic artifacts illegal in any national park, but it is disrespectful as well. Darwin Lambert, the first employee hired in Shenandoah National Park, in 1936, once wrote, "Cemetery seeking in this recycling park has been described as an exercise of high skill and empathy, a way of touching eternal realities of nature and humanity."

Prologue

ONE DAY, WHILE HIKING off trail in an area of Shenandoah National Park called Butterwood Branch—near where a tavern, a gristmill, a cider press, a schoolhouse, and an overnight stagecoach stop once stood—I lay down in the leaves on the edge of a rut in the earth that was once a wagon road, looked up at the silhouette of trees framing a damp gray sky, and decided to leave my office job of fifteen years and write this book.

My husband, Neil, our friend Jeremy, and I had spent the day bushwhacking, as we always do, sleuthing for backcountry cemeteries. We had succeeded in finding all three on our scavenger hunt agenda: the unmarked fieldstones buried inside a nest of greenbrier and graveyard myrtle near the junction of a decommissioned trail; the single carved headstone located miles into the skeletal winter woods where we sat for a moment's rest and were serenaded by a pack of howling coyotes; and the weatherworn marble obelisk at the end of a backwoods road trace barely discernible even by three sets of well-trained eyes.

Butterwood Branch, that magical place, is where we would go on to discover the largest dry-stack stone wall we'd ever encountered in the park, chest high and six feet wide at the base, moss and lichen covered, like liver spots on an aged hand—a fieldstone barricade that once kept in livestock, we presume, handwrought by some unknown master craftsman. Beneath the forest canopy, we uncovered an old spring, a rusty jalopy, and crumbling stone chimneys, plus a thawing deer carcass and tiny mouse bones on a rock. While hiking single file on a wide, grassy, old road—so surprisingly not filled in by trees or brush during its more than seventy-five years of disuse that it felt like the Yellow Brick Road—we scared up a rare golden eagle from its fresh, bloody great blue heron feast.

As I nestled into the soft ground, sounds of animal footsteps around me, cradled in the faded-blue folds of the gentle Appalachian ridges that have become my second home, I decided I wanted to write the stories of what I have seen, heard, touched, and discovered as a hiker in a de-peopled and re-wilded park—a place that was once unfound and then inhabited and is now "back to nature" once again.

I wanted to know what happened here, to feel viscerally the stories that would explain the headstones and shoe leather and washbasins and China shards that we have found throughout these wild woods. I wanted to know the place where the cabbages were bigger and the apples were sweeter, where the water tasted better and the air was cleaner, where you never had to lock your door and happiness was sitting out on a porch in the evening and listening to crickets. And even though sometimes you could see your footprints in the snow inside your own log-cabin house on the second floor, where the weather came in through the roof, the people who once lived here have said, "They were some of the best days of our lives."

Here, in this national park—in the mountains, in the country, away from it all—there is a tension. Most visitors don't feel it because they are blissfully unaware. They might notice an errant headstone, an old medicine bottle, even the exoskeleton of a broken woodstove by the side of the trail. But it can all easily be shrugged away. I did that too, for a number of years. I was fascinated but didn't ask questions. I learned a few facts along the way and drew fast conclusions. It's so much easier that way, not to know too much.

When I began asking questions of the park personnel, my words came out hostile. I made assumptions about people and motivations and the times. The story, as it seemed to me, was that a bunch of urban, privileged men in suits simply swooped in and muscled a few thousand self-sufficient farmers, orchardists, lumbermen, millers, and mountain tradesmen off their land against their will to create a national park, so that overworked Washington DC residents could enjoy a weekend playground, unfettered by the snaggletoothed riffraff.

In fact, the government did use its right of eminent domain to take land for the public good—in this case, for conservation and protection, for a national park, for the benefit of a nation—and paid the landowners, in exchange, money that some of the evicted residents thought so dirty and insulting that they refused to take it. Many of the landowners and residents—descendants of some of America's first pioneers—used the tools available to them in that era and culture and circumstance to try to fight back: leaving it to God's will, writing letters to decision makers, speaking to government staff, and in some cases, appealing to the courts. They didn't necessarily want more money; most just wanted to keep living the kind of simple life they knew on the piece of earth they loved.

They lost.

So did the landowners and residents who once lived in what is now Great Smoky Mountains National Park and a variety of other stunning federal lands throughout the nation, either through eminent domain or other land deals. They've been white, black, and Native people, all, in a spate of national conservation and commemoration on private lands from the 1930s to the present.

I knew none of this when I began hiking in Shenandoah. I hiked blindly for nearly two decades—group excursions with colleagues and friends, from the time I graduated from college until I became middle-aged; hikes motivated by views, peaks, and personal goals. It was a wild national park, after all. Green space, undeveloped, untrammeled, conserved; a concentrate of clean air, clean water, and quiet; species, habitat, and ecosystems: streams, wetlands, forests, high mountain ponds.

Once you begin to know something, though, you cannot unknow it, and over time, when I learned more of the story, I became more and more drawn to the people of the park—the ones who left and the ones who put their leaving into motion, the ones I sympathized with and the ones who drew my ire—with a particular curiosity for one man: William E. Carson, an unglamorous, long-forgotten cog in a wheel of Virginia history who seems the truest and staunchest driving force behind the project. A man who "has done more for the State than anyone who has not been Governor" with "a depth of vision and a strength of purpose that never have been adequately recognized." Based on the broad brushstroke of the story, it seemed he was responsible for all the unpleasantness of removing people from the park. He got under my skin. I wanted to know more about his motivations, his worldview, and what kind of man he really was.

And so I decided I wanted to visit the places of these stories purposefully, to search for the untold, the answers that would quell my growing discomfort of enjoying this misbegotten but beloved park. I wanted to backpack and bushwhack the backwoods, to the heart and soul of where the stories lived, to explore the hills and the hollows of the lost communities of Virginia's Blue Ridge Mountains, to know the people who once lived here and the men who determined their fate, and to discern for myself the justice of what happened here.

Shenandoah

⌒ All Souls' Day

"GONE," WAYNE BALDWIN SAYS of the large clapboard-sided, tin-roofed house that once stood in a hollow nestled among five mountains in what is now Shenandoah National Park. He has led my husband, Neil, and me down Hull School Trail and into thick brambles. We stand with a pile of large granite rocks at our feet, and an occasional brick, in a long rectangular gulley surrounded by a forest of towering trees.

"They knocked it down and burnt it up," Wayne goes on, smoking a cigarette, wearing a fleece vest with the national park logo. "This is where my cousins Beulah and Mary grew up."

The sky is achingly blue as we look up beyond the tallest tulip poplars, and the sun is filtering down to our feet through head-high bushes, casting camouflage shadows on our skin. Next to the house site is a bone-dry creek bed full of rounded rocks made red by soil, shards of pottery and a large glass jug, metal hardware that has grown thick with rust, and a piece of a horseshoe. Below the house site is a spring covered with a still-standing concrete archway, spilling out into a small run where Neil picks up a red eft salamander from under a rock and where, at a time when most mountain homes had no running water, Beulah Bolen, ninety years old, once did laundry in a stream-fed, gas-powered Maytag washing machine, heating water for it over a fire. "It took me just as long to get the crank going as it did to do the wash," she told us earlier in the day, about her early-twentieth-century youth.

Her sister Mary Bolen Burner—a feisty woman with tight white hair, elegant dark glasses, and a high-pitched booming voice—wanted to come down this steep trail with us, to show us the old home place herself, but the last time she did it, she said, "the way up reminded me that I'm eighty-eight."

What was once a massive eight-room frame house built in 1895, with two stone-and-brick chimneys, wall-paper, a telephone, and carved fireplace mantelpieces in five rooms, surrounded by apple and peach orchards and eight outbuildings, including a barn, a distillery later used to store wagons and buggies, a hog pen, a corn house, a meat house for drying and salting hogs, and a wagon shed where the family sheared sheep, has now been completely integrated into the forest. There is hardly any sign of this previous life left, and there's hardly anything any of us can say, standing around the haphazard rock pile. We do a collective head shake and then plow back through the brush to join the festivities up the hill.

It's September, the weekend of our anniversary, and as we do each fall, we're celebrating in Virginia's Blue Ridge Mountains, where we spent our first week-end together as young lovers after moving to the same state, where we cemented many of our early friendships, where we've gone repeatedly for recreation more than anywhere else, and where we were married many years ago. We are spending the day with Wayne Baldwin, a man we have never met. We are here to attend his family reunion.

It is an unusual family reunion, held here twice a year. His relatives come from as far away as California,

Oregon, and Washington, not to drive to a hall or a restaurant, not to cozy down with kin in a living room or backyard. They come to connect with the living and the dead, here at the Bolen Cemetery—once in the center of a private cornfield, now in the middle of the federal government's Shenandoah National Park.

The park's former backcountry, wilderness, and trails manager calls Wayne "quite a backcountry cemetery sleuth." Wayne is, in fact, the family historian. A tall, trim man in his fifties with a lean face, wire-framed glasses, and a head of thick but receding salt-and-pepper hair, he's been coming to the Bolen Cemetery since he was twelve. Back in the 1960s, a high school class project had him researching his great-great-great-grandfather, who drove an ammunition wagon in the Civil War, and his great-great-great-great-grandfather, who fought in the War of 1812.

Wayne Baldwin is no ordinary man. He is one of only a handful of park descendants who faithfully return to their ancestors' backcountry cemeteries, abandoned against their will in the 1920s and 1930s when the Commonwealth of Virginia condemned the land of a few thousand residents and paid what was considered just compensation so it could donate a chunk of the Blue Ridge to the federal government for a national park. Some of the despondent evacuees assumed that the cemeteries were off-limits, and so they never returned.

The National Park Service, the ultimate recipient of the taken land, has gone from conciliatory, to hard-lined, to somewhere in the middle, regarding cemeteries in national parks. In the 1930s, to help ease the pain of losing family cemeteries (at Shenandoah as well as the Great Smoky Mountains National Park and other places), the second National Park Service director, Horace M. Albright, issued a statement committing that "we will assume it is an obligation of the National Park Service to assist in keeping these cemeteries as cleaned up as possible after we have taken them over as part of the Park."

Albright also promised that those with family members buried there would always be allowed to come and go as they pleased, to clear brush and briars.

But no one explained these policies to the families, so few came. Today, for many of these sacred sites, there's not a road, not a path, that'll lead you to them. And if there were, you wouldn't find them pristine. Many are nearly obliterated, with obelisks toppled, iron gates mangled. Nothing takes down a burial ground faster than nature's demolition services: Virginia's verdant briars and creeping vines, its fires, bears, gypsy moths, and falling trees.

Albright's commitment to upkeep was honored until the mid-1950s, when the sixth National Park Service director, Conrad L. Wirth, determined that the park service was unable "to assume the full responsibility for the care of the cemeteries," which number more than a hundred in Shenandoah.

In 1964 Congress passed the Wilderness Act, which eventually restricted human activities in 40 percent of the park. According to the act, federal wilderness areas are "lands designated for preservation and protection in their natural condition" and areas "where the earth and its community of life are untrammeled by man." Wilderness areas throughout the nation can have no permanent roads, and roads that are already there are not maintained or are removed. Cars, chainsaws, and other mechanized equipment or machinery are prohibited. Not only do these rules make trail maintenance and other management more challenging for the agencies in charge, but any cemeteries in wilderness areas must be maintained by hand-tool-carrying, walk-in workers only.

In 1990 the cemetery directive changed again, withdrawing the park's gesture to furnish staff, equipment, or supplies for maintaining cemeteries and clarifying that the government would not now, not ever, build new roads to cemeteries that never had roads, like the many Neil and I have found by accident, off side trails, unmarked, overgrown with ivy and briars, in the middle of what visitors would now call "nowhere."

In the late 1990s the park determined that it was willing to work with recognized family organizations to establish cooperative agreements to assist in specific cemetery preservation projects, but ultimately, if families had not maintained their family plots in the past, "natural vegetative succession will reclaim the sites. No Park Service action will be taken to slow or abate this process."

Wayne and his predecessors have been avidly maintaining this particular cemetery for more than half a century. As far back as 1954, the park's chief ranger noted that of all the known cemeteries within the north district, the Bolen Cemetery "receives the most attention."

Wayne, in fact, has spent the last forty years of his life researching his family, tromping through the woods of Shenandoah National Park, where both sides of his family once lived and where both sides died. He trims brush and keeps the briars out of four family cemeteries within the park, three of which he travels to on foot, navigating what's left of the old wagon roads, concave ruts in the earth now filled with trees.

Wayne's family tree is complicated because a great-grandfather on his mother's side is the brother of a great-grandmother on his father's side, causing him to have relatives like a "double great-grandmother." He describes his relationship with Beulah and Mary as "my first cousins three times removed, times two; my second cousins two times removed; and my second cousins three times removed," all at the same time. Beulah and Mary's father and Wayne's double great-great-grandmother were brother and sister, and Beulah's grandfather and Wayne's great-great-great-grandmother (and, at the same time, great-great-grandmother—the same person on each side of the family) were brother and sister as well. Trying to draw this tree is nearly impossible.

Wayne's grandfather Oscar Baldwin was one of the landowners who took the state government's eminent-domain payoff money in the 1930s—$715, or about $9,440 in 2013, for his fifty-seven acres of steep, rocky land—and bought what he considered a better farm on better land, what some said was the opportunity of a lifetime. "$500 at that time . . . was, well, it was like opening King Tut's tomb," one former resident said. Wayne says his grandfather was not kicked off the land, like so many people said they were; he left voluntarily to make a better life elsewhere.

Records indicate, though, that Mr. Baldwin had asked about remaining on the land longer than his permit had allowed. "Special Use Permits," issued initially in 1934 to a few hundred residents who hadn't yet left their properties, gave former landowners and other residents permission to stay on their former land until the government could build resettlement homesteads for them, until they could secure new housing, or until they went on the welfare rolls.

The permit prohibited occupants from engaging in most of the self-sufficiency activities they had been involved in all their lives, however, like small-scale grazing and farming as well as trapping, tanning, and timbering—stripping bark for tannins to preserve leather and using wood for wagons, tool handles, mill wheels, shingles, brooms, and barrel staves—creating a somewhat untenable state. It was government land, after all, and you can't have the public doing anything they want on government land. The commonwealth issued a permit to Oscar Baldwin in 1934, and records indicate he remained on the land until at least November 1937, one year after the park officially opened to the public, which was far past the time that park planners had wanted the area rid of inhabitants. A letter from park superintendent James Ralph (J. R.) Lassiter reveals that after Mr. Baldwin asked about staying longer, he—like many others who sought more time on the land they loved—was ordered to vacate by January 1938.

Perhaps the difference in perception about whether Oscar Baldwin was kicked off the land or voluntarily left is simply a matter of Wayne's positive and conciliatory outlook. Wayne explains that he has always sought to hear all sides of the park eviction story. Even though his maternal grandmother was "real bitter" about the government taking her family's land—explaining, "I can't quote my grandma's exact words, but there was always expletives, and most of the time the government was called 'them s-o-bs'"—he says his father and others in the family felt no ill will. He continues, "One cousin said that even though people raised Cain and heck about the park coming, if it hadn't been for the park, most people would've ended up uneducated, inbreeding, and never left." On the other hand, Wayne says, "uprooting all those people that had grown up with each other, inter-married, and displacing them, separating them—I'm sure it was a fearful thing indeed."

Neil and I show up at the Little Devils Stairs parking area at 11:00 a.m., not exactly sure what to expect. We know it will be a potluck lunch buffet, so we have brought a thirty-five-dollar peach pie from the best pie shop we know of in northern Virginia. Can't go wrong with pie, we figure; it's not some new-fangled vegetarian dish, like Thai garlic green beans or blackened jerk tofu, which I might otherwise make for a potluck of my peers. I have never seen a pie that looked like this; rather than a crisscrossed lattice crust on top, the pastry crust is cut into serrated rounds that overlap each other all the way around the pie, except for a small circular opening in the middle to see through to the glowing orange peaches.

I feel self-conscious about not being related to anyone here, about not being related to anyone from the park, about being from the city—and a Yank. After the initial awkward greeting period, Wayne invites us into his s u v with his mom and cousin and takes off for the mile drive up the gravel fire road. We are a posse of about eight vehicles on a Do Not Enter park road. Rangers have unlocked the gate, due to Wayne's advance notice of the event and good relations with the park, but it feels illicit. Unlike most of our visits to this park, we're not here today to hike. We are not here to explore nature or to look for objects. We are here to honor everything that was lost to pave the way for our weekend-playground gain.

Neil and I first saw this cemetery back in 1992, within a year of moving to Virginia. I remember walking on a flat stretch of trail under a dark canopy of trees that were leafed-out in a deep forest green, after a strenuous hike up Little Devils Stairs, when suddenly, light-colored tombstones surrounded by a stone wall came into view. It was like a dream, in which unlike objects or settings or people that don't belong together appear in the same scene as if totally normal.

I had never seen a cemetery in a backcountry forest or national park.

I remember stopping to look at this unlikely relic, remember thinking the discovery was exciting, like finding an arrowhead or a Confederate button in the soil. We hopped the stone wall and walked among granite, marble, and fieldstones. With no other Shenandoah cemeteries to compare with back then, we didn't wonder why briars had not taken over the plot, why trees had not grown up inside. We didn't wonder who came miles into the woods on federal land and mowed the lawn.

Today, we get the answers to what we never thought to ask.

When we arrive at the cemetery with Wayne, everyone bursts out of their vehicles and begins assembling tables and lawn chairs and food. When I see other desserts showing up at one end of the spread, I set the peach pie out among them. Those who aren't working on fixing lunch are fanning out to place pots of fresh flowers at the grave sites of their relatives.

Wayne's mom places a bouquet at the graves of her grandmother and her "baby aunt and uncle," ages six months and one month. Mary and Beulah visit their grandparents, who purchased the family's thousand acres and built the Bolen house they grew up in here. They pay tribute to their mother, who died at age forty-eight, as well as to their baby sister, age three. Their father, who planted the twenty or so Norway maples that now shade the cemetery, is buried somewhere else.

Beulah—a gentle, quiet woman, delicate with soft features and pillowy skin—laments that her mother died when Beulah was just twelve, leaving her in charge of a family with seven children. Her childhood was full of work—planting and cutting down corn, gathering eggs, shearing sheep, milking cows, plucking geese for feather beds, making soap, cutting wood, and drying apples by spreading them on roofs in the sun.

She recalls the carbide gas lamps that lit her childhood home, an unusual fixture for a mountain house of that time, as many used beeswax candles and kerosene lamps mounted on walls. Her father would buy large hunks of calcium carbide from the store, which were placed in a five-foot hole near the house. The hole contained a tank that kept a gas—produced from the reaction of carbide and water—sealed and under pressure. She remembers pipes emerging from the hole, carrying the gas to fixtures in every room.

People start to introduce us to others, and eventually we are integrated a bit more into the group. Neil makes conversation with the only other person not related to anyone, a friend of the family. Neil explains to him that we are learning about the people of the park, the ones who had been displaced. "Displaced," the man spits. "That sounds like a Democrat word." Then he tells Neil that he believes the real reason why the people were kicked out was because the Blue Ridge Mountains were intended to be used by the government during World War II if the Germans were to attack the nation's capital, as a defendable position after Americans escaped to the west.

Outside the wrought-iron gate, when the tablecloths, utensils, and coolers are ready and the food is unwrapped, we are all called over to eat. One of the family patriarchs asks everyone to take hands and count off how many have joined here today (twenty-four) and to say grace. Then everyone digs in: mac and cheese, pasta salad, cucumber salad, baked beans with sausage, green beans, coleslaw, fried chicken, potato chips, and pimento cheese sandwiches (grated orange cheese with mayonnaise, chopped pimentos, and spices on white bread—a southern tradition). I had been worried I might not be able to find much to eat because I am a vegetarian, but my plate is full of delectable country cooking.

It's not too long before people start eating dessert. In no time at all, big hunks are cut out of the coconut cream pie, a hole is dug into banana pudding, brownies disappear, blood-red Jell-O is jiggling on flimsy white plates, and chocolate cake begins to vanish.

But nobody touches my pie.

⌒ Though I am antidevelopment and a conservationist, an avid lover of the national parks, and grateful for the drive and passion of the visionaries and planners who made this park happen despite all odds, the history of the land condemnation here has always seemed devastating to me.

Some people who left unwillingly refused ever to partake of the park. Some descendants say they feel horrible when they are there. Others, though, enjoyed the payment from the government—after the physical and emotional devastation of the Civil War; the decline of once-strong mountain-trade industries like tanning and handmade textiles, which succumbed to mechanized industrialization in lowland factories; the hard times of the Depression; the worst drought the state had ever seen; and the loss of the American chestnut trees, the economic workhorse of the mountains—and they relished the ability to start over somewhere else.

Beulah is the first living former resident I've ever met. In all our history-hikes up mountains and down hollows, bushwhacking through the past to try to understand what happened on these lands, examining the last vestiges of the eighteenth- and nineteenth-century English, German, Scots-Irish, Irish, French, and Swiss settlers who once made their homes here, Neil and I have never really heard from a living, breathing survivor. When I ask how she felt upon hearing the family would have to move away from their home, from the rolling fields and wide sky that can hardly be pictured now under the shadow of the forest canopy, whether her family was content with leaving, she shrieks, "No, indeedy! We cried like babies!"

"It really wasn't better," she explains calmly. "We were moved over there, and we didn't have no fruit, and the water was hard. Over here, we had a great big spring, and we could collect it in a bucket to drink. We once had all kinds of orchards and nuts." She was fifteen, and Mary thirteen, when they relocated to the town of Sperryville, about six miles away in the lowlands. But when asked if the memories of what happened to her have made the park too painful to enjoy during the long years of her life, she says with her slow southern drawl, stoically, befitting of someone with the wisdom of time and age, "Well, you get over that."

I eventually notice that each dessert maker has cut slices in advance to get people started, and so finally—in my tormented, self-conscious state—I walk over to my beautiful, untouched pie, grab a knife from another dessert, and make some slices ready to eat. Cousins hovering near the food table begin congregating around me as I work.

No one's engaging with me. I am sure they don't remember my name. But soon a woman named Robin inches toward me from behind and leans in close. "Everyone is talking about that pie," she whispers in my ear. "No one makes that kind of pie anymore."

Still slicing, I feel a smile creep over my face in quiet relief. "My grandmother used to make a pie like that," she says, referring to the overlapping pastry-rounds design. "But no one since."

I set down the knife and step away from the table, only to have the space I inhabited filled instantly with eager pie eaters. I had hit the jackpot. Robin and several other people take huge wedges of it.

At cleanup time, there is still about a third of the pie left. I would love to have more of it, but I approach Robin, who has warmed my day with thoughts of her grandmother's lost tradition. "Do you want the rest of this?" I ask. Her eyes widen. "I'd love it," she said.

At the end of the picnic, we are all hugs. Mary and Beulah and Robin bid us a fond farewell, and Wayne and his mom gush about how nice it was for us to come. I don't have words to convey how grateful I am that they took us in to the folds of their family—the joyous day as well as the painful past. For the nearly two decades we have been tromping around the hills and the hollows of this magnificent place, feeling like interlopers, we have never gotten this close to the real mountain residents, the flesh and blood of history.

They have put faces to the stone foundations and rock walls we will continue to find. They have put names to the unmarked graves to which our future hikes in this park will no doubt lead. Despite my own inner maelstrom, they have let us know, with their acceptance: *It is alright that you are here.*

～ A Cabin in the Woods

ONE HUNDRED MILES FROM the nation's capital, west of the stone monuments commemorating freedom and democracy that rise up from the city's coastal bog, beyond the nation's bloody memories at Manassas Battlefield, past where the Piedmont Plateau meets the first ripple of the Blue Ridge foothills, to the first ridge of the accordion folds of the Virginia Appalachians, there is a place called Jones Mountain. It is a spur ridge, jutting out like an appendage from the main northeast-southwest spine of the lizard-shaped Shenandoah National Park, with two high points, draining northward into the Staunton River valley and southward into the Conway.

Inaccessible by road, high above the nearest town of Graves Mill, and tucked away at the head of one of Jones Mountain's many hollows is a former mountain man's home, a fifteen–by–twenty-two–foot, two-story log cabin with a massive hand-built stone chimney: the Harvey Nichols place, or as we know it today, the Jones Mountain Cabin. The cabin is a relative secret but known by avid hikers as the most remote rentable cabin in the park, a seven-mile-roundtrip backpacking adventure.

It's March, and Neil and I are making our way there to live the life that was lost, to live simply again, to live as everyone lived when the place was built in 1855, when it was considered a small but choice, middle-class rural mountain property—one of thousands of homes in dozens of "neighborhoods" that once dotted the mountainsides.

Accessible only by foot either from Skyline Drive—the narrow road snaking one hundred miles through the park at the highest points on the ridge—or from the lowlands to the east, the cabin is neighbored by nothing but two hundred thousand acres of public land administered by the National Park Service. The Skyline Drive route is an up-and-down journey traversing other mountains and passing through nearby gaps. The eastern route is a steady uphill climb gaining 1,200 feet in elevation. We're taking the latter, the approximate path Harvey used thousands of times when coming home from town, hauling in corn meal and wooden barrels for his distillery, a "son of a gun place to get to," as one of his neighbors used to say.

I haven't always been interested in survival recreation. I grew up a city girl who spent little time anywhere featuring chlorophyll, water coming out of the ground, or panoramic open space. I knew the best falafel joint in Philadelphia, in an underused part of the city, in an alley near the gay and lesbian bookstore, but I couldn't tell you whether the stars were out the night before or if I'd ever seen the Milky Way. I spent high school afternoons on the rooftop of my twenty-story apartment building downtown—gravelly and sticky, black and pungent under my soles in the summer sun—smoking pot with my friends, but I'd never seen a waterfall or scrambled up rocks for a view of a landscape.

Today, I'm hauling a backpack of thirty pounds with everything I'll need to survive the cold weekend on the mountain, a place without electricity, heat regulated by a thermostat, running water, or flushing toilets. The Potomac Appalachian Trail Club (PATC) website says that the hike to Jones Mountain Cabin is "long" and "difficult," but I am not too alarmed, actually. Hiking to a well-stocked PATC cabin is what I'd call backpacking light. We don't have to bring a camping stove, fuel, pots and pans, dishes, utensils, a tent, sleeping pads, axes, or saws, because the cabin is supplied with kitchen wares, thin mattresses, sleeping platforms, and tools.

Most of the weight is food; we like to eat nearly as well as we do at home when we are camping. Harvey would slaughter a farm animal for dinner, and his wife or daughter would pull turnips from the garden. We, on the other hand, are prepared for breakfasts of home fries and oats with cinnamon honey and morning coffee; lunches of cheese and crackers, pesto, nuts, and dried fruit; and spaghetti and burritos for dinner. We also carry a backcountry first-aid kit in case anything goes wrong, soap and sponge, sleeping bags, warm clothing, rain gear, and a stash of toilet paper for the outhouse. Compared to pitching a tent and digging holes to squat over, this isn't really roughing it, but it's not entirely the Four Seasons either.

This country is different from any other area in Shenandoah National Park we've ever been in. The mountains seem higher. Rather than hiking a long way to a mountain far off in the distance whose size is indiscernible, on this hike the full height of Jones Mountain—bare and browned by winter—is next to us the entire time as we circle around it from the bottom. The trees are taller and straighter here, massive tulip poplars growing straight to the sky without much underbrush beneath them, like giant toothpicks. The river is rushing and deep, and for a while, the old-road trail is pristine, as if someone has used a leaf blower to clear it of all debris. Bright-green club moss, an ancient plant whose flammable spores were once used as flash powder in photography, lines the trail.

We hike a gentle ascent for about three miles riverside; then the final mile includes the steepest stretch. This part of the trip is a narrow foot trail, a diversion from the stock paths and wagon roads, clearly hand cut, meandering through young mountain laurels with their smooth, shiny, evergreen leaves, steep enough that looking straight ahead means fixing your gaze on the ground where you'll place your next steps. This is where Neil chugs up the trail and barely breaks a sweat while I begin cursing and wondering why I'm here, whether this agony is worth whatever experience I'm about to have.

But I plod on. A few minutes of complaining helps pass the time. After the no-pain-no-gain hill from hell, we hit the junction to the Jones Mountain Trail, where water trickles out of rocks and wets the trail, and we enter the tallest, thickest, biggest stand of mountain laurels either of us has ever seen. At about twelve feet high, they form a tunnel over us like a Roman arch, and their trunks are as wide around as my thighs, in their twisted broken-leg type configurations. They form an impenetrable wall on either side of the trail for about half a mile and seem infinite in their spread across this mountain. We are high above the Staunton River valley now, and at an overlook along the way, we can peer out across it to the peak on the other side—not a house, not a mall, not a car, not a soul in sight in any direction, which is why people like us come to a place like this.

Then, standing on a rise, we turn away from the overlook and begin a descent into Harvey's hollow. In a clearing, like a dream unfolding in real life, the tiny log cabin—nearly camouflaged against the dull, brown-gray winter vegetation, where a short, stocky man with a thick, pointy mustache once made his home—comes into view.

From the vantage point of a rocking chair on the rough-hewn front porch of the chestnut-timber log cabin in winter, a visitor can see a rushing spring twenty-five feet to the right, pouring from the slight ledge in the ground with such force that, after filling a pot with water, you might catch yourself reaching to turn off the nonexistent faucet. It is the only water source for cabin residents. It is also the beginning of a narrow creek headed down toward the confluence of the Staunton and Rapidan Rivers, and it is the only place to bathe. To the left is a steep rise up to a plateau covered with gnarled, muscle-bound mountain laurels, the other side of which yields the rocky drop-off into the Staunton River valley, a wide V-shaped opening between Jones Mountain and Fork Mountain that makes me feel I could be out West.

Straight ahead, to the east: bare ground, picked clean by visitors foraging for firewood, like a scene out of *The Lorax*, in a secondary or tertiary forest of oak and black locust that was once predominantly American chestnut, and in the long-distance view toward Graves Mill: a parting of the canopy. When visiting the privy at night with the door propped open to take in the blazing Milky Way, you can see the twinkle of a single house or car several miles away in this direction (or, I imagine, perhaps a far-off intruder with a headlamp pushing through blackness and brush). Behind the cabin: nothing but thick, thorny brown shrubbery and twisty vines, an impassable hillside.

Those are the views that most visitors see.

Me—I can't help myself; I only see the past.

When I sit on the front porch of Harvey's home, I see the springhouse to the right, a roofed wooden structure where the cool pooled water from the earth creates a mini refrigerator and keeps the family's milk and eggs cold. Behind the springhouse are the confetti colors of bean, corn, and rye fields, and below the spring, a hog pen made of solid walnut. Harvey's moonshine still, a homemade apparatus involving a copper kettle, copper tubing, and a barrel, where he makes rye whiskey and tangy apple, peach, and blackberry brandy—legally until Prohibition—is chained to a nearby tree. And there's a path disappearing into the woods where he carries equipment to another stream and hollow nearby, under the glow of the moon to continue his trade illegally, out of sight of the revenuers.

To the left and around back, I am surrounded by the dark, knobby arms of apple trees and the glint of orange fuzz on peaches—Harvey's vast orchard, which serves as his liquor-making raw materials. Somewhere up on the rise at left, an open flat in my mind's eye, I see a white headstone and footstone next to a peach tree—the grave of Cricket Nichols, Harvey's second wife. Behind the cabin, a barn and two animal sheds for hogs, sheep, chickens, and cows, plus two horses and a mule to help with plowing; a vast acreage of surrounding forest; and blackberry and rose bushes, carefully tended, around the perimeter of the house.

Straight ahead are the delicate, trellised plants of a vineyard and a kitchen garden full of cabbages, potatoes, snap peas, and green beans, and a sixty-two-tree apple orchard just beyond.

Unlike today, when this little Eden is a quiet and preserved forest, shaded by an umbrella of regrowth and only visited by the hearty few willing to backpack here, Harvey's reality in the late 1800s and early 1900s featured an active working farm and business. There, a man and his three successive wives and seven children lived off the land, where customers traveled from all over Madison County up Jones Mountain—they'd drive as far as they could and then walk—to purchase "Harvey's Special," what was known as the region's finest whiskey, even by the county treasurer, and where the world was as large as the distance a man could walk in the full length of a day.

The cabin itself has not changed much since then. Surrounded by hardwoods, the house's chimney and cooking fireplace are the originals, built by Harvey's father, as are the stone foundation and wide chestnut timbers. Concrete has since replaced mud as the mortar between logs and stones. The roof has been redone. The porch no longer runs along the entire front of the house. The basement, now a tool cache, is no longer a livable space. But the essence, as you open the solid wooden door into the cold, musty, two-story, two-room house, remains, thanks to the Potomac Appalachian Trail Club, which found Harvey's cabin in 1937 just a few months after he had despairingly vacated it upon park orders and again in 1968—roof caved in, abandoned for more than thirty years—and rehabilitated it for the pleasure of hikers.

The first time I backpacked, in the High Peaks region of the Adirondacks, just three months after Neil and I began dating when I was a senior in college, I cried.

I understood the idea of hiking all day with all our supplies on our backs, spontaneously finding somewhere to set up our tent and sleep, and hiking some more the next day, but I could not envision—and thus had not factored in—how it would be to carry all that weight while hiking uphill and scrambling over boulders. I did not know that the backpack would leave indentations in my collarbones and black-and-blue marks in my armpits.

I did not know that the trails in the High Peaks region would still be covered in snow and ice in May, that I'd be balancing myself on slippery precipices with dramatic drops, in the rain. I did not realize that I'd be so sweaty during the day and that when it all dried, I'd be so cold at night. In the end, I had never worked so hard or walked so far on such difficult terrain.

Neil—who had lived off the land with two friends in British Columbia for a winter and lived ruggedly for seven years as a seasonal U.S. Forest Service surveyor in Middle-of-Nowhere, Idaho—could not have predicted my difficulty of putting one foot in front of the other in the forest.

In Center City Philadelphia we didn't have to push ourselves physically beyond our comfort zone. Mom and I took a cart to the grocery store so as not to tire our arms out on the way home. We cabbed or bussed or subwayed if a walk was too long. The extent of my athletic life was going to gym class, which I detested, and learning how to throw and catch a ball in the park. I never even learned how to ride a bike. My life had never required any real ambulatory skills, and not until I had lived two decades did anyone I meet even suggest such activities.

A science and outdoor educator and naturalist, a hiker and backpacker, a birdwatcher, and somewhat of a loner, Neil finds joy in scanning the skies for hawks and black vultures, turning over rocks looking for salamanders, or searching for some kind of hornwort slime on a log. He's someone who likes to get away from it all, who finds the simple rituals of finding a place to camp, feeding ourselves, collecting water, and working to stay warm the richest and most satisfying of times; everything else is just business.

We met; I was in love; what else could I do?

And so I backpacked. Again and again. In that twisted love-it-but-hate-it kind of way, in that I-don't-have-anything-better-to-do kind of way, and in that I'm-the-girlfriend/wife-of-this-hiker-and-naturalist-so-I'd-better-get-with-the-program kind of way. I wanted to be the rustic, outdoorsy, woodsy person that Neil encouraged me to be, and eventually I became some version of it, hoofing it from Great Smoky Mountains to Craters of the Moon to Death Valley.

In college, I had majored in natural resources because of my interest in saving the environment, the *it* topic of the 1980s that I latched onto in high school as a biology-interested budding activist looking for a cause. But I had never really seen the landscapes or ecosystems I was interested in protecting. I had never laid eyes on geological anomalies or wildlife—twisted red-rock canyons, underground volcanic tubes, desert lizards, and squeaking bats. These sites were so far from my world of art deco apartment buildings, contemporary glass edifices, and the underground tunnels of Philadelphia's subway trolley that Neil could have just as easily taken me to Mars.

My patient mentor taught me about gear and equipment, like how to pack a backpack, use a backpacking stove to cook real meals, and set up a tent. He helped me buy my first pair of hiking boots and the backpack I still use today. He showed me how to treat a blister, ford a stream, read a topographic map, and use a compass. He explained how weather generally moves in from the west, showed me how to build a fire, and demonstrated how to negotiate wild animals, like when a full-rack bull moose blocked our trail while backpacking in the River of No Return Wilderness in Idaho or when a wild stallion galloped into our camp at a national wildlife refuge in Nevada. In drenching rains in Shenandoah and high-altitude lightning in New Mexico, in the back recesses of American wilderness, where we lay curled together in our mummy bags in the tent with the ground trembling, waiting for weather to pass, Neil taught me about attitude—about patience and reward, quiet and risk.

Eventually I would see that my formative years in my historic city had been quite relevant after all, that they had nurtured a particular interest in me that would form the backbone of my new hiking life with Neil. It was an odd fascination that might have lain dormant if not for Neil and his persistent curiosity about nature and the wild.

Spawned at Independence Mall, in the parlor of the future Dolley Madison, in the basement of the home site of Benjamin Franklin, and within the fenced grounds of Christ Church Burial Ground where Franklin and other founding fathers are entombed and where I spent weekends in the 1970s with Mom reading every last acid-rain-washed marble tombstone, line by line, it had grown in me undetected. It was, simply, an attachment to the past, a longing for days I never knew, and a fascination with the search for stories that can be found among stone.

Indeed, I didn't realize this curiosity resided within me until I moved to Virginia—Revolutionary War country, Civil War country—and until I found myself in the middle of Shenandoah National Park, nearly twenty years ago, standing in those woods of towering maples after hiking seven miles in complete solitude, gazing upon an incongruous, well-maintained cemetery in the middle of the forest.

Someone once lived here, I realized then. This was a community. This is not just wilderness; this was a destination on a map.

On that day, my love affair with this park began.

What I have seen here in Harvey's woods—the remnants of human habitation—is, in fact, the end of the Shenandoah National Park story. Families lived here, worked here, raised kids here, and died here for two centuries. Their kin were removed from the land, and now there's a park.

I had always taken this place for granted, this retreat where Neil and I spend weekends and vacations, camping and hiking. I had never considered there were consequences from the creation of national parks. Neil had taught me that national parks were good, that when everything around you is paved and subdivided—indeed, if every last inch of natural America were to be built upon—you would still have the national parks, pockets of refuge in a country that is full of painful views. He had showed me that the national parks are the pride of the nation. But once we began finding more and more remnants of human habitation in the woods, I began asking myself if he was wrong.

The men who made the decisions about the fate of Harvey's land reduced his property to two-dimensional surveyor marks on paper, a cold appraisal of the value of buildings and timber, and a slip of pulp called a deed, rolled up in a piece of legislation written in legalese giving the government permission to take it all away. But the roots of private ownership of Jones Mountain run deep, and the land held more stories than one man could tell.

Harvey Nichols's domain had been part of the 5.2 million–acre land grant from King Charles II to the ancestors of Lord Fairfax in 1649; a slice of the thousand acres purchased by the river's namesake, Thomas Staunton, in 1726; a section of 350 acres owned by a couple named David and Elizabeth Jones, who purchased the land from the colony of Virginia in 1741 but were found scalped to death on the top of their eponymous mountain; and a parcel of 3,000 acres owned by Tom Graves in 1784, for whom the nearby town of Graves Mill is named, a fourth-generation descendant of a captain who settled at Jamestown in 1608.

By the time an artist named George Catlin, who traveled west beyond the Mississippi in 1832, first conjured up the idea of national parks, the land on which Jones Mountain Cabin sits had already been bought and sold by English and Scots-Irish settlers and in private hands for nearly two hundred years.

In its lifetime during those years, the area of Jones Mountain, just one peak of many in Virginia's Great Mountains, as they were then known, had been used for grist mills, grazing, farming, orchards, tobacco plantations worked by up to fifty slaves, investment property, and as a buffer against additional development and subdivision. Even then, men were purchasing lands to preserve their views.

By 1872 when the U.S. government gave the OK to the concept of national parks and Congress set aside part of "its own" federal lands (bye-bye Indians) to preserve forever the beautiful, freakish landscape of Yellowstone National Park—the nation's (and the world's) first national park—Harvey Nichols's great-uncle had already moved to Jones Mountain. He had purchased 120 acres for the price of four hundred bushels of rye and had sold the land to nephew Albert, who built the original Jones Mountain Cabin and fathered Harvey in 1866 after returning from the Civil War.

Seeing what was happening out West by 1890—Sequoia National Park, Yosemite—leaders in the tourism industry and the conservation movement in North Carolina began clamoring to protect their own natural wonders: the southern Appalachian virgin forests being logged into oblivion. They petitioned Congress to establish a park or forest reserve in the southern Appalachian Mountains.

Fifty leaders from seven southeastern states came together to discuss the vision of a southern Appalachian national park, while Harvey walked up to fifteen miles in a day to call on women, looking for a wife.

In 1901 two bills appropriating millions of dollars to purchase millions of acres for an Appalachian park were introduced in Congress. According to a *Sierra Club Bulletin* from 1903, "the park has received favorable indorsement [sic] from forestry experts, from the Secretary of Agriculture and the Secretary of Interior. President [Theodore] Roosevelt also sent a special message to Congress, asking that body to favorably consider its establishment."

While Harvey was courting and marrying his first bride, Eula, from Pine Grove Hollow, and fathering four children on Jones Mountain in the first decade of the twentieth century, the idea of the southern Appalachian park flatlined, was revived, and then died its same death again, though the western parks continued to flourish with the latest new creations: Crater Lake in 1902, Wind Cave in 1903, Mesa Verde in 1906.

Perhaps lawmakers had a sense of how difficult the task would turn out to be, or perhaps in the continued prioritization of projects involved with running the country, it just never measured up to other needs. Perhaps, in the words of Bruce Babbitt, the secretary of the interior under President Clinton, this southern Appalachian national park concept just did not yet have the "one committed, passionate, pain-in-the-ass person who perseveres," which he said is behind every new national park.

In 1915—the defining year for what writer Wallace Stegner called, "the best idea we ever had," or the beginning of the end if you happened to be Harvey Nichols, living in the East on a piece of private land the government wanted—the U.S. Department of the Interior hired someone to create the National Park Service as a new government agency. Stephen T. Mather, avid hiker and millionaire borax manufacturer, sparked a media frenzy about national parks.

Mather, a "human whirlwind," had complained to the secretary of the interior years earlier that he didn't like how the parks were run, and so he was invited to come to Washington to develop a park system and fix them up himself. He financed cushy trips with air mattresses, linen table cloths, and wait staff for leading scientists, writers, and congressmen to visit the natural wonders.

His efforts paved the way for the 1916 creation of the new federal agency, finally bringing together under one unit all of the nationally preserved lands that had been accumulating due to the diligence of the country's leaders, a system that now includes 90 million acres of land and water in 392 parks. Its mission: the preservation of wildness.

Western park designation continued (Denali in 1917 and Grand Canyon and Zion in 1919) while the old idea of a park in the East—to round out the park system, to give people someplace they could easily drive to in the new age of automobiles, to usher in a new era of land use by turning privately owned agricultural land into free, federally managed recreation areas for everyone— was being tossed around in Mather's head.

Harvey was already fifty years old, his black mustache turned white, when two small eastern parks came to pass. When Acadia National Park in Maine was donated by a group of wealthy individuals in 1919, to conserve what they feared would be ruined by development, and Hot Springs National Park in Arkansas, also in 1919, was created from land already held by the federal government since the early 1800s, Harvey had already buried Eula, dead from childbirth, as well as his father Albert.

No one had yet pinpointed Harvey's place on the map, but these small eastern parks came nowhere near rivaling the size and stature of those in the West.

And so the foreplay continued.

When we arrive at the cabin, living like it was 1900 is no longer theoretical—we are immediately plunged into Harvey's life. As in Harvey's day, our chores are defined by our gender and completed in relative silence.

The cabin is cold, so Neil sets to work making a fire in both the fireplace and the woodstove to warm the building, using wood left by the previous renters. Because they didn't leave enough for one night's use, per PATC protocol, however, and because we need more for the coming days, Neil collects a set of tools and heads off into the woods to look for fallen trees and limbs, something dead he can drag back to the cabin. When he returns, he lays the hardwood logs and limbs on top of the old stump of a chopping block out front, saws them to fireplace- and woodstove-lengths, then sets them upright and splits them with the ax, demonstrating the saying that wood heat warms you twice.

Harvey, of course, would have known his land much better than Neil does; Neil has had to scour the hillsides for some time to come back with an adequate haul. From his daily work in the garden, farm, and still and from his walks to visit friends and women in other hollows, Harvey would have already noted in his mind where to come back for a supply of good wood. This activity would have been rote and necessary twelve months of the year.

While Neil is off doing man-work, I—as Harvey's older daughters or wife would have done—make house. I set out our bedding pallets provided in the cabin and make a sofa of sorts and two sleeping areas. I light candles to bring a warm glow to the otherwise dreary interior—the cabin's three small windows do not bring in nearly enough light. I move furniture around so the two rocking chairs are near the fireplace, and I hang our food in a pest-proof location outside. I grab the largest pot I can find and collect water from the spring to boil for cooking, cleaning, and drinking. I rinse all the kitchen wares I think we'll use, to remove mouse droppings and fire soot, and then I begin preparing for dinner: set the table, pull out ingredients, and chop vegetables, with the tiny Swiss Army knife Neil gave me for my college graduation a decade and a half ago.

Harvey's girls would have been much more accustomed to this lifestyle, which for them wasn't just a lifestyle but also their livelihood. But I am somewhat afraid of cooking in the fireplace—pulling the red-hot grate down from its hinge, fire lapping against the sides of the saucepans—so Neil winds up doing some of the cooking as well.

Unlike in Harvey's day, we use a water filter for any unboiled water we consume, to prevent contracting the parasite giardia, which can live in streams and springs. We come prepared with multiple layers of modern fabrics like fleece and polypropylene to keep us warm, and ultimately, unlike Harvey's family, which rarely had a day off from the work of their everyday lives, we have come here—to this national park, to this cabin in the woods maintained by a hiking club—for recreation.

But it takes all day to live here. By the time the cabin has been warmed to a habitable temperature, we have finished cleaning the pots, cooking, eating, and cleaning again. We have stacked wood in two places inside the cabin, I have bathed myself from a pot of warm water by flickering firelight (a luxury, I imagine, in Harvey's time, with so many people in the house and so much work to be done), and we have bedded down for the night on wooden platforms, without a round of Yahtzee, without reading to one another, without any backcountry romance, on opposite ends of the cabin—not quite sleeping (we have to stoke the two fires about every hour) but resting our weary bodies. From our lives near Washington DC, a two-hour drive and a three-hour hike away, it has taken us a long time to go so far back.

~~ While Harvey, a single father, toiled to provide for his four daughters by fishing, hunting, butchering, and preserving food, keeping up his trade in whiskey, which increased quite a bit after Prohibition in 1917 ("You could go to Jones Mountain and get apple brandy faster than you could get a glass of water," rancher Bob Smith once said), new National Park Service director Stephen Mather, in a parallel universe in Washington DC, was hard at work on the southern park.

After thirty years and six presidential administrations, Mather was finally someone who believed that the United States needed an eastern equivalent of Yellowstone or Yosemite, needed a place where most of the people of the country lived, in order to keep the National Park Service funded, to keep the agency viable to continue its mission of conservation. By 1923 he was inundated with requests for new national parks by cities and states in the East wishing to increase tourism and preserve forests. Thirty-two mountain cities and towns became active in the movement to establish a national park in their home territories. Riding on the backs of the proponents of this park idea over the years, Mather—whom the nation would memorialize by naming Mather Point in the Grand Canyon, Mather Pass in Kings Canyon, and Mather Gorge in Great Falls near Washington DC—became the first man to make these dreams come true. He believed in the vision of a large national park in the southern Appalachians, and his boss—Dr. Hubert Work, the secretary of the interior—agreed.

Work created a committee composed of five men who were nationally known experts on parks and outdoor recreation; its task was to scope out a site.

While it considered twenty or so site suggestions for where a southern Appalachian park should be located, based on a survey it had distributed, Virginia's Shenandoah Valley grassroots park-promotion machine sprung into action. "A national park near the nation's capital" became the rallying cry of local Virginia businesses and politicians, whom some believed organized themselves with more gusto than had been seen in the commonwealth since the Civil War. But what better to motivate a group of businessmen than a prediction that "the sum total of new wealth brought into the Valley . . . would be beyond computation."

It was a local, small-town campaign involving men with a single-minded big vision. Leaders wanted to boost the area's economy and raise money for roads and other infrastructure to lift up the commonwealth from its torpor. They wanted to profit from the park, in the present and in perpetuity, and see Virginia shine.

On the mountain, though, Harvey continued living his ordinary life, getting by. He had already heartily survived the influenza epidemic of 1918. He had rebuilt his cabin—and himself—after his beloved home burnt down. "One fire will ruin a man," Harvey had told his daughters. He felled all the chestnut trees he needed to build himself a new cabin and a new set of furniture.

He had courted and married his second wife, Cricket, a young brunette with black button eyes from nearby Devil's Ditch in 1920. She joined him at the cabin, where aside from cooking all day, building fences, and taking care of the children, she enjoyed summer evenings on the front porch playing mountain ballads on the banjo for her family and friends.

In 1922 on a hot June evening, when the twenty-six-year-old love of his life gave birth to twins and then died—"a terrible night; the worst suffering that I have ever witnessed," according to his daughter Minnie—Harvey buried Cricket next to the peach tree on the flat above the cabin, wanting her close to his house for the rest of his life. Before marrying his third young wife, Cricket's sister, and fathering several more children, he spent the next decade living alone.

Not too far away, a thousand Virginia delegates—strangers to Harvey—attended one of the first meetings about the park. They formed a regional chamber of commerce with a thirty-member board of directors. They also inspired the formation of a park-related association, with a short, mustachioed, and flamboyant local man named George Freeman Pollock as president.

Pollock wanted the government to locate the park in Virginia; and specifically, he wanted it to be sited along the first ridge of the Blue Ridge Mountains. Even more specifically, he wanted it to surround and support the mountain resort that he had built on land he had sort of inherited from his father but that had plunged him into huge debt: Skyland—"the most unique resort in the U.S." and "the only dude ranch in the Eastern U.S.," according to its letterhead in the early twentieth century, adorned by a logo of a cowboy on horseback.

Pollock—a salesman who would spin any tale necessary to get what he wanted—had convinced a court in 1900 to let him buy his father's and his father's partners' failed copper mining land on credit, selling off building lots to vacationers to make the payments. A man who was known for yodeling and building bonfires that could be seen from miles away and who, as a boy in Washington DC, longed for wilderness so much that he kept live owls, flying squirrels, and a raccoon in his attic, Pollock dreamed that a national park in his backyard could turn his fortunes around and tell the world about his mountain mecca.

He submitted a copy of the committee survey in a bid to bring the park to his doorstep. He, like everyone else involved with the project to date, mentioned nothing about the people living in the area, going as far as stating that the area was "absolutely free" from commercial development, even though the land was dotted with mines from as long ago as the Revolutionary War and at least 40 percent of the potential park consisted of farms, orchards, or pastureland. He did not even consider his own business establishment of fifty cottages, a dining hall, a post office, a rifle range, and tennis courts to be a mark on the landscape.

Buried in a fat paragraph about notable trees and wildlife in the area, he did note, "There are within this area, of course, a few small mountain farms, of no great value." He admitted at some point that perhaps 1,500 mountain residents would be put out of their homes if the project came to pass. Other estimates said as many as 15,000 people, or about 1 percent of Virginia's population.

No one batted an eye.

To woo the committee to select the Virginia Blue Ridge as the park site—Virginia found itself in competition primarily with the Smoky Mountains of North Carolina and Tennessee—the Virginia governor, a state senator, and others accompanied committee members on hikes and horseback rides within the proposed park. Pollock built towers on high points, blazed new trails and bridal paths, and collected letters from influential guests. He hosted dinners and conventions, inviting photographers, furnishing horses for dignitaries and naturalists, and preparing lavish and aromatic meals to coincide with committee members' returns from cold and wet explorations.

After considering dozens of potential locations throughout the East, the committee was swayed by the Virginia team and the Blue Ridge's location within two hours of the nation's capital and 40 million Americans—a third of the U.S. population. In May 1926 Congress passed and President Calvin Coolidge signed a bill to authorize the secretary of the interior to accept a minimum of 250,000 acres and a maximum of 521,000 acres for Shenandoah National Park in Virginia. Coolidge gave the go-ahead for Great Smoky Mountains National Park to proceed as well.

There was one condition in the bill: the federal government would buy no land. The Commonwealth of Virginia would have to gain titles from the landowners—the nameless and faceless mountaineers whom no one could envision protesting, whom no one could envision suing in a court of law, whom no one could envision refusing to leave what many outsiders considered their godforsaken, hardscrabble homes—then donate the deeds to the federal government. Though it could not know about the protracted battle that would ensue, ending with arrests and Civilian Conservation Corps boys torching families' homes—"the matter of moving the people out will take care of itself," one park promoter had said—Uncle Sam washed its hands of the dirty work.

⌒ The next day of our trip consists of all the tasks associated with cooking, cleaning, chopping, and splitting all over again; a little bit of relaxation on the porch with a book and some yoga; and a short hike up Bear Church Rock for long-distance views across the ridge. Despite the emphasis on manual labor, a weekend at

Jones Mountain Cabin soars by, whether from sheer enjoyment or wishful thinking.

On our final day, after eating our oatmeal, after cleaning out a pot caked with oats using hot water and a few drops of liquid soap, a messy job for the front porch of Harvey's house while trying to prevent dumping microtrash over the rails, and before emptying the cabin of our belongings, filling in the guest registry, sweeping, and stacking new wood for the next inhabitants, I insist on one last task before we leave: finding Cricket. Thus we begin the long hunt, as we cannot tell from the history books whether the grave is to the right, left, or back of the cabin—just that it is on a hill.

Although winter obliterates the obstacles that fully sprouted leaves pose to finding structures like cabin foundations and chimneys, the accumulation of undecomposed leaves on the ground obscures anything at your feet. Picking through a maze of vines and thorns, we scour each hillside until we find the right rise. We slush around in the leaves looking for a headstone for a good hour, searching for Harvey's beloved, whose final resting place Harvey was forced to abandon, along with his home and business, in 1937, two years after the park officially opened to the clamoring public. After years of refusing a federal government resettlement homestead in some lowland town—"If you take this place, I won't live much longer . . . I don't have the strength to start all over," he said—he hung his head and accepted the $8.33 per acre ($137 per acre in 2013) compensation for his land and moved to another home on another mountain, where he died seven years later at age seventy-eight.

After forty-five minutes or an hour, I am ready to give up this search. Even Cricket's great-great-grandson noted in the cabin journal that he could not find her resting place. I know she's here, that she lived and loved on this land, that her kind spirit pervades this little hollow and watches over this house—visitors to the cabin often report signs of her ghost—and I am content to walk away having tasted for a couple of days the life she once lived with the man she loved, deep in this pocket hollow of forgotten time.

But as is often the case on our bushwhacking excursions, Neil prevails. With his infinite patience and methodical search system, he finally spots the headstone and footstone—long, thin, unmarked rocks plucked from the earth, poking out of the ground as described, a depression in the earth, and four thin, dark logs forming a rectangle on the ground around the grave, a recent enclosure made by another enamored visitor, covered over in forest duff.

In this moment, Jones Mountain's past and present are alive again as one. In my mind's eye, I see the black-and-white photograph of Cricket from one of my history books—a cherubic little whisper of a thing in a white knit hat and wool coat at age twenty-one at a mountain mission nearby, where she helped peel apples for drying until midnight one cold November night, 1916. We take a moment to think of her, paying respects to a woman we never knew, imagining her life here on this fallow hillside. Simply because we are here, we are witnesses to a life once lived.

And then in the still silence of the morning, just the sound of bare branches strumming up against one another and the trill of perhaps a cedar waxwing, we hitch our packs onto our backs and retrace our steps through the tunnel of laurels, boots slapping down against the steep trail on our way back to the road.

The mountains call us here because of what was lost, what was taken, what is gone. The hollows and hills here in this jewel of America are rich, not just because of what is here, but because of what is no longer here. In our history-hiking journeys, we try to capture the essence of that absence, ingest it, embrace it, make it ours, make it come alive, bring the people back, finding remnants of their lives and inhabiting their space. But on our way back home, when we have to leave it all behind, when the folds of the hollow consume Harvey's house like the night closing in upon the day, as we head lower and lower into the flatlands and back toward the city, and as the mountains fade into their shades of blue, the people of the past are all just as gone as ever.

The park, and nothing else, is what's left.

Bushwhack

LONG JOHNSED AND POLAR FLEECED, wool hatted and lug booted, we prepare for our hike under a chandelier of stars. It's twenty degrees, and we're headed out on a different kind of adventure. Instead of taking a trail, a blazed path that's cleared of brush, leveled, and marked on a map, telling us where to go to reach a destination; instead of following a stream up or down a mountain to a peak or a waterfall; indeed, instead of scaling Old Rag Mountain, that heart-pumping killer of a climb over a heap of ragged boulders, as we have enjoyed and endured numerous times throughout two decades, Neil and I are hiking to a place few have ever been—the lost neighborhoods of Old Rag, a bushwhacking exploration through the hollows and valleys below the mountain, to survey the remnants of home sites left in the woods.

The hike we are not taking to the top today is not insignificant. Old Rag Mountain—a lone, shaggy buffalo against a plain when seen from a distance, a monadnock in geological terms—is its own ridge, apart from all the others. It is the most popular hike in Shenandoah National Park, with one hundred thousand people—about 10 percent of Shenandoah's annual visitors—climbing it each year. They are university and church groups, Boy Scouts, hiking clubs, and packs of young, urban professionals, mostly from the Washington DC metropolitan area, and they are willing to hike more than nine miles, for at least six hours, over difficult terrain, in any weather. Not for the timid, a climb over this geological anomaly is, for many, a rite of passage.

Hikers usually start on the Ridge Trail, which begins as a well-used dirt path through oak-hickory forest lined with mountain laurel and switchbacks up the behemoth nine times in about two miles, a substantial climb for anyone who hasn't been using their elliptical machine. Then it reaches the beginning of the rocky area that gives this massive hunk of granite its original name: Ragged Mountain or Ragged Top. It is there that hikers must start working the rock.

Old Rag requires as much upper-body strength as it does powerful legs and cardiovascular fitness. You must lower yourself down into a two-foot-wide crevice that's six feet deep and then heave yourself up from that same crack a few feet later. When the next step of the trail is a sheer face with a ledge at eye height, you must climb up using barely there handholds and footholds, crude and ungraceful and animal-like. On crowded summer days, a line can begin to form in this obstacle course—like the Hillary Step on Everest. Slogging through rock instead of through mud, like some kind of hiker boot camp, takes many hours.

After completing the full 2,200-foot ascent, the summit awaits, which is actually quite anticlimactic—just the end of all the hard work before the beginning of a mildly rocky but generally easy bipedal downhill hike.

In fact, in the five or six times I've completed this hike, the return has always been rather disappointing, a regular earthen trail leading to a junction with the Berry Hollow and Weakley Hollow fire roads, the latter of which hikers slog along for three miles. I had thought for years that this wide, gravel swath is not only the longest, most boring part of the Old Rag hike, but it's the most tedious part of any hike in the entire two hundred thousand–acre park, after such a high.

There was much I did not yet know about this road.

⁓ The rock that sits atop this isolated peak, Old Rag Granite, is a billion years old. It's been crumbling down to the valley in chunks for thousands of years. For hikers, these chunks are obstacles, climbing surfaces, trail-building materials, seats on which to rest, and moonscapes to photograph. For the community that began forming in the area in 1750—European settlers who had sought a new mountain home in a new land, a place to build a better life—these pieces were free building materials, stacked to support the very first house.

When I first started coming here, I didn't know—as most people don't—that in the shadow of this ragged feature, a network of old roads crisscrosses the base of the mountain. I didn't know that if we had stood on that same ground in 1900 or 1930, we would have seen clapboard homes; a rainbow of fruit orchards; the bulky machinery of farms; fence-enclosed gardens; active gristmills grinding corn and wheat; a stave mill for barrels used for shipping apples; the work of stonemasons, carpenters, basket makers, and blacksmiths; and one of the most vibrant communities in all of the Virginia Blue Ridge—a town called Old Rag Post Office, or Oldrag P.O.

I didn't know that someone like Mattie Yager's parents met in this hollow, at one of the big dances families used to have, part of all-night apple butter boiling parties. The whole community would gather, and people would take turns stirring apples in a kettle—forty or fifty pounds of them—for at least twenty-four hours so they didn't stick. "Once around the side and twice through the middle," stirrers would sing.

"They'd clear out a big room and dance all night long," Yager explained years later. "There was a flap dance to the floor. They didn't waltz . . . this was really hoe-down dancing." If the boy stirring allowed the paddle to touch the side of the kettle, she said, "you had to kiss the girl. That's the way my father got acquainted with my mother."

I didn't know that families dug trenches around their homes here and filled them with straw to preserve cabbages, turnips, and potatoes in the ground through the winter. That they logged, tanned, operated legal distilleries, tended orchards for cider or brandy or apples, and collected ginseng root to sell. That they raised hogs, had blow-out hog-killing parties with spiked lemonade, and then cured the meat in their own sheds. That there was never a weekend that passed in the Yager home when Mama didn't make chocolate pie, custard pie, butterscotch pie, and coconut cake from scratch.

What I didn't know for so many years as I slogged over that gray gravel fire road, bemoaning with buddies the dreariness of the return, was that Weakley and Berry Hollows were once considered home and that the stone skeletons of people's lives remained.

Today we are bushwhacking the underbelly of the mountain.

Not cutting our way through the woods with a machete, but traveling off trail, navigating thickly brushed-in backcountry. In all the years I had heard my husband talk about this activity, it had always sounded macho and aimless, something guys would attempt just to see if they could do it, a way to make a hike more challenging. I never felt any interest in bushwhacking for its own sake, when we could more easily take a trail.

Now we're using a bushwhacking field guide of sorts, written by an avid Virginia hiker named Leonard F. Wheat. Wheat's book is a guided bushwhack through the hollows below the mountain. It navigates the "experienced, well-conditioned hiker" using fixed features such as boulders and streams, historical landmarks such as stone walls, hard-to-see topographical features such as ridges, objects no longer there such as hemlock trees (which succumbed to the woolly adelgid pest in the late 1990s), and a network of old road traces, often just hardly discernible concave ruts in the earth. It is a metes and bounds survey, if you will.

We will use Wheat's hand-drawn, not-to-scale maps of nine roads of the old-road network he has uncovered in the woods, long abandoned, and we will conduct our own census of sorts, a postmortem survey of the remains of eighteen remote cabins Wheat has charted.

Bushwhacking "season," as Wheat puts it, runs from November 1 to April 1, when the rattlesnakes have denned, when the ticks are more dormant, when the poison ivy and stinging nettles have withered, and when the leaves have fallen from the trees, thus providing clear viewing of the visible and invisible overland routes the book describes. The best time, therefore, is in the depths of winter. Neil and I do our Old Rag excursions in December of one year and March of the next. For most people, this is the off-season: there are no fiery leaves, blooming mountain laurels, or delicate pink wild azaleas. The sky is icy, and the forest is brown, brittle, and lifeless. And yet for us, out here in the nothingness by ourselves on a journey of discovery of the past, it is all so alive.

In the spring and summer of 1927, another man led another type of survey on these same lands. William

E. Carson—the man selected by Virginia's fiftieth governor, Harry F. Byrd Sr., to head the newly created State Commission on Conservation and Development—led a group of men in surveying nearly four thousand tracts of private properties being considered for Shenandoah National Park.

Civil engineers fanned out into the field and into courthouses to conduct a tract-by-tract census of the approximately 521,000-acre area envisioned for the great southern Appalachian park. They walked up stone or wooden steps to log and clapboard homes and measured and assessed the condition of each real-life house, barn, and outbuilding, noting building materials and condition, and they talked to the real people of the mountain, who lived the joy and hardship of their everyday lives there. Foresters marched through woods and jotted down notes about the number of fruit trees and the types and value of commercial timber. Carson put out $10,000 ($130,000 in 2013) of his own money to commission the U.S. Geological Survey to produce eight hand-drawn maps of the area, based on what his men had found. Together, they and land appraisers formulated an initial assessment of the market value of the land. They wanted to know what it was worth. They were planning to buy it all.

During their visits, the surveyors told the residents of generalized plans for the coming park. They suggested that people sell their land early. They provided rudimentary information about timeline and process, as nothing had yet been decided, and thus they unintentionally started rumors swirling. They noted, "Men over 60 years old are generally loathe to move," and "Grazing land owners do not wish to sell their mountain pastures." Though some of the landowners did sell—providing about eleven thousand easy acres for the park—some residents did not understand what was happening. Many weren't interested in selling their land for any price. A few indicated they would take up arms.

With this history as our backdrop—Carson's maps are the basis for Wheat's property-by-property route—our first act of anarchy is at the trailhead, where everyone else heads south, destined for the top of the mountain, while we take off to the west. When Wheat gives us the cue, we veer off trail and head into the woods at the north flank of the mountain, and his words lead us to what he calls "Old Road," the first of the mountain secrets revealed.

Despite the thick blanket of leaves on the ground, the abandoned road is easy to see once deep inside the forest. It's wide, slightly depressed, and outlined with rocks on both sides. This particular road was never suitable for cars—only wagons; in fact, the postmaster and storeowner who lived in town is known to have traveled seven miles out of the way around the mountain on a different road to fetch supplies because he couldn't take his car on this one.

Finding the road is one thing, but traveling the road is quite another. Because no one has maintained this transportation route for more than seventy years, nature has overtaken it. Small trees have grown up inside it. Logs have toppled over it, and fallen branches have filled it. Rocks that once lined it have rolled into the gulley. Untouched by humans over so many years, it has simply integrated itself into the forest, been swallowed up by everything that lives and sprouts.

I want to walk inside the road as much as possible, for the full experience of reliving the past. But this is even more arduous than staying on its edges, which aren't cleared either—full of devilish greenbrier ("blasphem weed") and blackberry and raspberry thorns, as well as large pits in the earth from areas where trees have uprooted—and I have to detour from it frequently to move forward.

During one of these detours, I spot an eight-by-ten-foot rectangular stone box surrounding a spring, with water seeping naturally out of the earth—a place unknown even to Wheat, making me feel like an archaeologist uncovering a buried tomb. Groundwater that has traveled through cracks and fissures of rock, sometimes from quite a distance underground, pours or trickles out of these natural faucets, and residents who depended on them for drinking water, for cleaning, for watering animals, and as a source of cool refrigeration, often built rock walls around them. The walls created small pools, identified and protected the sites, served as the base for small wooden sheds that covered the pool to protect milk and eggs stored inside, and prevented the water from becoming buried or contaminated.

The four sides of this spring box—like all the ones we've ever seen in this park—are brick-like walls made from fragments of Old Rag rock, each stone carefully chosen for its flat rectangularness, its ability to be stacked and lined up with all the others and form a solid structure. The enclosure uses no concrete or mortar, just the sheer weight of one well-placed rock on top of another with the flair of an experienced mason. What the box tells us is that we have found a place of habitation.

Moving on through the woods, we soon come to the landmark Wheat calls simply "Stone Fence," a four-foot-high intricately and perfectly built dry-stack rock wall spanning nearly a quarter mile in virtual obscurity on the other side of Brokenback Run. This wall—Andy Goldsworthy-esque, a light-gray stone giving way to the dark gray and green of crisp lichen and spongy moss, within a hundred feet of the well-trammeled Weakley

Hollow Fire Road but something no hiker would ever see from that trail—likely marked a property line or kept farm animals from running free when this area was cleared of trees. A work of "outsider art," it's one of the many utilitarian sculptures that the men of the Blue Ridge made that turned their mountains into museums.

Crawling under fallen logs and hoisting ourselves back up, stomping through brush that scratches me deeply enough to draw blood through my pants, swatting away the branches aimed at gouging out our eyes, we continue through the understory of the forest, searching for a "gullied side road at a backwards angle" and other cryptic, nearly invisible spots: clues to finding three of the eighteen cabins formerly owned by the estate of one of the many ordinary men who lived in these mountains. (Survey Notes: Tract #39, 169 acres, owned by the estate of J. O. Sisk, including five main buildings, 15' x 32' shingle-roofed frame house in fair condition, 19' x 30' x 16' shingle-roofed frame barn with 8 other outbuildings, 65 apple trees, and stands of oak, hemlock, and poplar.)

With made-up street names for all-but-made-up routes, Wheat's writing is outrageous, and I often feel lost in the landscape that has changed in the fifteen years since the guide was published. Yet an hour and a half from when we started, after methodically following Wheat's convoluted instructions, we see the rock pile that is our first clue that people once farmed this land (they, as farmers still do today, cleared rocks out of fields and piled them here and there), then the foundation of an outbuilding, and then Ridgeside Cabin itself—a rectangular rock formation built into the ridge side, just where Wheat says it will be. We kick up three washtubs here, ubiquitous throughout the park, either white porcelain-covered metal basins or white and blue together, like

early twentieth-century spin art, or plain gray metal—
cheap items usually rusted and bottomed out, left behind
when families abandoned their home.

Plowing through the woods like raiders of the lost
ark, a little smug and holier than thou compared to the
lemming hikers up top, we don't find Concrete Cabin
but check off Chimney Cabin—a big crumbling brick
chimney at the edge of a creek with a mature tulip
poplar growing inside what would have been the living
room. Nearby, Neil decides to sit down and rest amid a
bed of periwinkle (also known as graveyard myrtle)—
those dark, shiny, oval leaves traditionally planted at
gravesites—and our eyes are instantly drawn to the con-
trast on the hillside: a long, thin, solitary white fieldstone anchored into the dark earth. We know at once
that it is marking some unknown person's final resting
place, which I can't imagine will ever be found again.

The never-never land we find ourselves in—a place
that once was and will never be again—reminds me of
something Mattie Yager said in the 1970s, years after
her parents were gone, years after the family left the
mountains. "Oh, I'd love to have went over there but
I never could have," she lamented about a place such
as where Neil and I happen to find ourselves at this
moment, land lost to the ages. "I couldn't walk up that
mountain, and you couldn't get up there in a car. Now
I think about all our ancestors; grandmother and all of
their children and everything buried up there. I just
wonder if it's all growed up. I reckon that you wouldn't
even find the cemetery."

This, I suppose, is exactly why we are here.

To continue, we follow directions like "Go uphill along
the e rim of the gully (Old Road). Where it curves w, it
immediately comes to a rocky creek bed. Do not cross
the creek. Pause to look s e uphill. See where a hemlock

woods that has been on your left (E) ends. Go s uphill, staying on the E side of the creek. Soon come to a 5-ft high boulder . . ." and navigate our way to Two Boulder Cabin (SURVEY NOTES: TRACT #42, 37 ACRES, OWNED BY WILL N. WEAKLEY, INCLUDING FIVE MAIN BUILDINGS, 16′ X 18′ SHIN-GLE WEATHERBOARDED HOUSE WITH SIDE ROOM IN FAIR CONDI-TION, 15′ X 15′ SHINGLE-ROOFED LOG BARN IN POOR CONDITION WITH THREE ADDITIONAL OUTBUILDINGS, 30 APPLE TREES AND NO MERCHANTABLE TIMBER), a stone foundation surrounded by daffodil greens—bulbs that continue to flower each year for decades or possibly even centuries—and a variety of historical trash: a corked liquor bottle, mason jars, and a bottomless blue porcelain pot. We hit Rock-pile Cabin and then head uphill toward Walls-Up Cabin (both part of Weakley's same tract), which, according to Wheat, is the best of the eighteen cabins because, as its name suggests, it and its nearby henhouse still have walls, unlike all the others.

When we arrive, though, the vertical space that Walls-Up Cabin ought to fill is empty; the walls are gone. Those that have not been incinerated into dust or ash lay as charred sticks on the ground, like a skeleton without a body. Arson, we learn later: two fires that destroyed some of the only log architecture here not already destroyed upon creation of the park. Rusty springs of a mattress sit inside the burnt structure, while hikers yowl in the crisp air atop the mountain; and despite the fire, the story that nobody knows hides beneath, in plain sight.

⁓ Though a federal land endeavor, managed by a national agency in the end, Shenandoah National Park was really a state project. Many local Virginia men were involved with the idea over many years—conservationists, businessmen, politicians—and many would receive credit.

Ultimately, though, Shenandoah came to be because of the persistence of William E. Carson alone. Governor Byrd, a close friend, chose him for his doggedness; for his success in life as a lawyer, a state senator, and the president and general manager of his father's lime company (the company that built the entire Front Royal, Virginia, region, adjacent to the park); for his service to the nation, encouraging banking reform and helping to create the Federal Reserve System, promoting mining safety and scientific research by helping to create the U.S. Bureau of Mines, and becoming president of the National Lime Association. And, no small matter, he had gotten the governor elected, as Byrd's campaign manager.

The governor also chose him for his philosophy in how to build up Virginia. Carson did not believe in developing the state in the traditional sense of smoke-spewing industrial factories. Rather, as one researcher put it, he believed in "using Virginia's past to vault her into the future," to use conservation of the commonwealth's natural and historic resources as a means of development. Tourism, he believed, should be the state's main industry, and the governor agreed. "A satisfied visitor is our best investment," Byrd said.

Over the course of his service in the state commission, Carson would create the entire Virginia state park system, opening the first six of what would become thirty-five state parks now visited by 7.5 million people a year. He would lead the effort to install a siege of highway markers to commemorate historical events and sites throughout the commonwealth, which can now be found in 2,200 locations in Virginia—and in many other states that followed his lead. He would establish the ten thousand–acre Colonial National Historic Park, including preserving historic Jamestown and the Yorktown Battlefield and creating a parkway that connects the two to Colonial Williamsburg, hosting 3.3 million visitors a year. He would also be the first to request funding and thus take the initial step toward building what would become the Blue Ridge Parkway, to connect Shenandoah National Park with Great Smoky Mountains National Park.

And he did it all without pay. "There is no higher conception of duty than to feel we are of service to the State," he once said—the very echo of Robert E. Lee.

Carson accepted the challenge of surveying and mapping the land to determine ownership, boundaries, and value. He agreed to ensuring the appraisal of properties, raising and managing the money to buy them, and acquiring the land. His role was to manage the park affairs, all the ordinary and extraordinary details that would come to be involved with the project. He was so confident, when he assessed the situation in 1926, that he said the park would open within a year.

It opened a decade later.

Not everything went as planned. When his surveyors returned to the office, they reported that the area wasn't quite the wilderness the park promoters had depicted in their early bid to get Congress to locate the park in the Virginia Blue Ridge: the area encompassed 5,650 tracts and 3,250 homes, and purchasing it all would average $15.30 per acre.

Original fundraising campaigns had assumed a cost of $6 per acre—the *assessed taxable value* of the land rather than *market value*. They had called in public relations firms from New York and initiated a "Buy an Acre" campaign. Solicitors had scoured the state, swaying 23,000 citizens to pledge $6 to "buy" one acre of future park, but the organizations had only collected about two-thirds of the pledges. Despite the ultimate donation of fairly large sums from the likes of John D. Rockefeller Jr., park planners had only collected a fraction of the total goal of $2.5 million.

"If a bomb had been exploded in the room, scarcely more consternation would have been created among the commission," is what records of an August 1927 meeting indicate about the news of the actual cost. Carson and his commission began to press donors to send in the payments they had pledged, and they began discussing with Secretary of the Interior Hubert Work the idea that the park acreage might have to be reduced.

Then Carson led a second survey. This time, the results were even worse, with land values estimated at an average of $21 per acre.

Carson asked the governor to appropriate a million dollars for the project to supplement donations. At the same time, the commission considered abandoning the national park idea entirely and creating a state park instead, not only because of the money problems, but also because antipark activists began noting that much of the so-called primeval, virgin forest had actually been cut over for industry about every three decades for the last two hundred years and had become quite good open grazing land instead. (In 1927 the U.S. Department of Agriculture had even acknowledged that these mountains were some of the most important beef-producing areas of the United States.)

But Carson convinced Secretary Work to allow Arno B. Cammerer, then assistant director of the National Park Service, to survey the park for a third time and to choose some areas to leave out of the boundary. Indeed, Cammerer recommended cutting back the approved acreage of the park from 521,000 acres to 327,000 acres (only 3,800 tracts), removing some of the fertile hollows and pricy lowlands ("We must cut our cloth to fit our available funds," Carson said), though the area still encompassed approximately sixteen thousand people.

Still, no one had involved any of the residents in the decisions or asked them if they wanted a hand in shaping their own destiny.

"The commission has attached to its large staffs not a single man with any authority who might possess the point of view of the landowner," one editorial in a local paper read.

With the new boundary line established, Carson developed a plan for a "quick and speedy" set of arrangements, noting to the men of his commission, "There will be no persuasion or bullying," he wrote in a memo, "just a cold business matter by which we can scientifically and mathematically submit exact valuations on the land."

But the survey crews had discovered that many landowners did not own proper title to their land or did not know where exactly their property boundaries were. Records had been lost during the Civil War when courthouses were burned down. Many of the claims on the land went back to the days of Lord Fairfax, who had been granted land in the 1600s by the king of England and who had established a land-leasing system that spanned numerous generations but that had become complicated when the Commonwealth of Virginia began selling the land to leaseholders in his absence. Unused land was often thought of as common land, and courts sometimes had decided that even longtime squatters became owners after using the land a certain number of years.

The men also learned about tenants, residents who did not own land at all but whose families had been living on and working the same land for numerous generations. In a centuries-long custom, off-site owners often allowed tenants to live on and work their land. These tenants did not pay rent nor owe any portion of their farm or timber products to the landowner; the owner benefited by having free caretakers of their land and cabins. Sometimes owners inherited tenants from previous owners; the tradition was to keep the same tenants on the land even as ownership changed hands, meaning that the tenant families often knew the land better and felt more deeply attached to it than the landowner.

Adding to the complications, by the early 1930s, due to the repercussions of the Great Depression and the great Virginia drought, many large contributors had begun reducing or withdrawing the fundraising pledges that park planners had counted on. At the same time, the state threatened to rescind its million-dollar appropriation.

But Carson was devoted to the project, so he convinced Congress to reduce the park's minimum boundary yet again, from 327,000 acres to 160,000 instead—a fraction of its originally proposed size. He was forced into a saw-toothed, zigzagged boundary—"a jigsaw puzzle of mostly low-value tracts"—to avoid the pricy fertile areas and include less-prized rocky areas. While Great Smoky Mountains National Park fulfilled the conservationist-activists' original vision of a huge expanse of protected southern Appalachian forest, Shenandoah ended up as a "fish skeleton."

∼ Our attempt at the next eleven cabins takes us into the heart of "town," but it is a ghost tour, really, because nearly everything Wheat points out is no longer there.

His words lead us to the Old Rag cemetery, with its thin, asymmetrical, unmarked white fieldstones popping out against club moss and the dark leafy ground, hidden in the forest—sixteen graves in three rows, with deep depressions in the earth the length and width of coffins, indicating their decay. Thousands of hikers pass it on every trip down the mountain; most, like us, have never noticed it.

He directs us to the site of the old John W. Butler country store (TRACT #87, 122 ACRES OWNED BY JOHN W. BUTLER, WITH FIVE MAIN BUILDINGS INCLUDING A 25′ X 25′ WEATHERBOARD HOUSE IN FAIR CONDITION, A 16′ X 22′ 8′ SHINGLE-ROOFED LOG AND FRAME BARN IN POOR CONDITION WITH THREE ADDITIONAL OUTBUILDINGS, 72 APPLE TREES, AND WHITE AND YELLOW PINE WOODS), at the junction of trails and fire roads where a National Park Service information kiosk now stands, and to the site of the United Brethren Church (TRACT #227, 0.25 ACRES, WITH A 20′ X 29′ FRAME BUILDING IN FAIR CONDITION), behind which in 1911 the neighborhood kids would sneak to play poker.

We stand on the place where the 1919 log-cabin post office and a shop for provisions once stood, owned and run by Mattie Yager's uncle, William Austin Brown, a thin, white-bearded, bespectacled, suit-jacketed, cane-carrying postmaster who bartered on behalf of residents when he made his trips into town: Eggs for coffee, perhaps? Chickens for sugar?

Farther on, we find the spring box, root cellar, and rock retaining wall of what is believed to be Postmaster Brown's log-and-frame shingled home (TRACT #52, 36 ACRES WITH SIX MAIN BUILDINGS, INCLUDING THE POST OFFICE/STORE, A 28′ X 12′ SHINGLE-ROOFED LOG AND FRAME HOUSE, 33′ X 14′ SHINGLE-ROOFED LOG BARN IN POOR CONDITION, ALONG WITH SEVEN ADDITIONAL OUTBUILDINGS, 30 APPLE TREES, AND NO MERCHANTABLE TIMBER); an old jalopy with a tree growing through the middle of it and nearby Jalopy Cabin (TRACT #48, 44 ACRES OWNED BY ELMER DYER WITH FOUR MAIN BUILDINGS, INCLUDING A 19′ X 19′ AND 12′ X 18′ SHINGLE-ROOFED LOG AND FRAME HOUSES IN FAIR CONDITION,

A 25′ X 25′ SHINGLE-ROOFED LOG BARN IN POOR CONDITION
WITH FOUR ADDITIONAL OUTBUILDINGS, 80 APPLE TREES, AND
NO MERCHANTABLE TIMBER); a heap of rocks that could be
the bulldozed remains of a school; and four other cabins. Everywhere, like garbage strewn on the ground, we
are surrounded by the rock of cabin foundations, root
cellars built deep into the earth, and retaining walls:
human creations from nature's stony discards. Wheat's
words—his painstaking on-the-ground documentation—
show us the world within a world and offer a secret passageway into the past.

Our last jaunt on this around-the-mountain journey,
a detour from the boring old gravel road, along a mostly
obliterated, nearly invisible abandoned side road, takes
us to a site that is as ordinary or as extraordinary as
the others: the site of two foundations—a house and perhaps an outbuilding like a kitchen or shed, which Wheat
calls Northwest Cabin (TRACT #38, 432 ACRES OWNED BY
H. F. HUDSON, WITH THREE MAIN BUILDINGS, INCLUDING A
16′ X 24′ SHINGLE-ROOFED FRAME HOUSE IN FAIR CONDITION
AND A 14′ X 36′ X 12′ SHINGLE-ROOFED FRAME AND LOG BARN
WITH FIVE ADDITIONAL OUTBUILDINGS, 64 APPLE TREES, AND
A STAND OF OAK AND HEMLOCK). When we return to this
particular site two weeks later, after a hike up to the
mountaintop on New Year's Day with friends, bringing
them here for a treat on the way down, I get an unexpected glimpse into the past.

A good friend of ours has organized this outing with
his buddy Kent. Kent tells us he's been hiking in this
park, on this trail, for more than half his life, though
he doesn't know much about the flora and fauna, geology, or history of the area. He seems somewhat interested in hearing about what I know. When we arrive at
Old Road, after descending the mountain and passing
through the ghost town of Oldrag P.O., I point out the

stone pile where the school once stood and the path toward the jalopy. Kent seems to perk up with this new-found information, though he can't get his mind around why anyone would settle here, or if they did, why they would stay—never mind that the Old Rag valley in particular was well watered and extremely fertile and that the settlers enjoyed the mountains because they were reminiscent of home. But in any case, he's soon curious enough about odd-shaped rock piles the size of suvs, a five-hundred-foot rock-wall boundary line, three tiers of rock-wall terracing up a steep hillside, and foundations built into the hillside, that we begin traipsing back into the woods together to examine things close-up.

When we arrive at Northwest Cabin, Kent is no longer content just to view what I show him; he's off searching the entire area around the cabin footprint on his own, pushing through branches, thorns and all, to see what he can find. In less than ten minutes, he leads us to three large, intact steel pieces of an old Southern Oak woodstove, a few footsteps downhill from the cabin site.

I admire it and praise him on his finding abilities. Always nice to culture a new protector and empathizer, I think to myself.

Then he says, "Do you consider this to be a pristine site?" I ponder this question for a second. Well, how could it be? Dozens, if not hundreds, of people have been here before. Not sure of what he's getting at, I say no.

"Then I guess it would be ok for me to take home a piece of this stove," he says and starts toward a piece of cast iron. I quickly inform him that it's illegal to take anything from the park, including what the park service calls "historic trash." In all our trips to national parks throughout the years, we have been well schooled in the rules about removing artifacts—Indian historic trash, cowboy junk, wildflowers, and even rocks. We are sticklers for leave-no-trace hiking and camping: take nothing but photos, leave nothing but footprints.

"Plus," I implore, "then you would remove the joy of future discovery for other people."

"Aw, then they can come to my house, and I'll only charge them a dollar," he laughs. "The two of us will come back here when you're not around," he says, then turns back to the trail.

"Not funny," I mutter.

I keep a good distance from Kent on the rest of the way to the car, crushed with my inability to foresee the possibility that I could be leading a fox directly to the henhouse and desperately sad for what might unfold.

Aside from meaning "to hike off-trail through thick woods and brush," *to bushwhack* also means "to ambush; to wait in hiding to attack; to strike suddenly from a place of concealment." Here, I feel bushwhacked. It is, in micro form, how I imagine some of the people who lived on these lands might have felt, living in what would become the war zone of their lives.

Carson, after all, was working on his coup de grâce—a final solution for taking the land from the people for the park. In addition to the money problems and the boundary problems, Carson complained about the arduousness of having to acquire land from so many different people, one by one, in the thousands. "The work up to this time has been child's play compared with what we have ahead of us," Carson told his commission during this process. "The amount of work . . . is paralyzing."

Instead of individual, private transactions with each buyer, Carson convinced the Virginia legislature to pass a blanket condemnation law in 1928. This law would allow the state to take all the properties at once, in each of eight counties, by right of eminent domain: the right of the government to take property for public use as long as just compensation is paid. Eight cases instead of thousands.

"It was manifestly hopeless to undertake to acquire the necessary area by direct purchase [because] any of the thousands of owners or claimants could hold up the entire project unless paid exorbitant and unfair prices, with jury trials, appeals, and all the endless delays which can be injected into ordinary condemnation proceedings by selfish, stubborn and avaricious litigants," he said. Instead, he'd bulldoze them all together.

Convinced that this act was constitutional, that it would avoid the dreaded jury trials, appeals, and endless delays, Carson—a man who believed that dignity was one of Virginia's greatest assets—ensured he would not be thrust into any face-to-face contact with the potentially avaricious landowners.

When the residents heard of these plans, plans to remove them from land that was as close to the heart as a blood relation, they may have felt bushwhacked indeed, as if a machete had cut a swath through their very souls.

I think back to what Mattie Yager once said of her mountain relatives: "Them people lived good. They lived happy and they lived good. I expect that they lived happier up there in the mountain than they are living now. Because out here in this here world, it seems to me like, well, I'll just say, everybody is for theirself, and the devil is for them all."

Just like Carson and his commission, and the governor and the state and the local business community—all of whom acted as though the mountain people, the mountain homes, and the mountain culture were dispensable when they decided on a park location without considering the residents or including them in deliberations—Kent can come back and steal that old rusty metal if he wants; no one will ever know.

Thankfully, though, I come to this: neither Kent nor Carson can destroy the rock, that divinely created, impenetrable time capsule that will always rat out the tale. It is all laid bare on Old Rag Mountain: square, round, brick-like, dry stacked by hand in piles and rectangles, columns, and terraces. White crystals. Blue quartz. Red garnet. It is as old as the days of continent forming and ocean making and mountain building, long before the beginnings of insignificant man. It is impossible to ignore. It is the inanimate embodiment of this neighborhood of souls. It is the voice of all those who once toiled and frolicked and fought and loved and bore children on these lands. It is—fortunately for descendants of Shenandoah and history lovers and those who value what once was—what neither ignorant hikers nor powerful governments can destroy, here in the dark valley in the shadow of the great mountain.

Hollow Folk Hollow

IT IS THE FOURTH OF JULY, and we decide to visit Corbin Hollow, to witness for ourselves the scene of the crime: where Americans—in all their "all men are created equal" and "life, liberty, and pursuit of happiness" glory—slaughtered, in words, all the residents of this hollow.

What we know before we come here is that in the 1930s, Washington DC science writer Thomas R. Henry wrote a collection of now-lambasted articles in the *Washington Evening Star* and elsewhere about the people living in the Blue Ridge Mountains of Virginia.

"The depths of ignorance and squalor found in isolated clusters of mud-plastered log cabins . . . hardly can be exaggerated," he said.

"Hidden communities of backward, illiterate people living in medieval squalor . . . illustrat[e] the effect of both degenerative cross-breeding and difficult environment."

"The basic fault lies in the character of the people themselves."

We know, too, that in 1932 Henry and so-called sociologist Dr. Mandel Sherman, PhD, MD—director of the Washington Child Research Center, associate professor of education psychology at the University of Chicago, and a scientist who published in peer-review journals—published findings in a now long-discredited book called *Hollow Folk*. The book reported on a study, carried out "under conditions close to laboratory control," of five communities in and around what became the park, which, according to the authors, "present five stages of culture."

At the highest level of social development, the authors write, is a proper town called Criglersville, in a valley at the edge of the mountains, where Dr. Sherman lived, where paved roads lead to "a progressive school in a modern building," "newspapers are received every day," "regular working hours are maintained," and "all the common American games are played."

At the next highest level, they describe Richards Hollow as a "socialized" community at the foot of the mountains, where the people are "cleaner and better dressed than in the other three communities" and "express their thoughts in more meaningful language" and "can read and understand newspapers" as well as "the Bible, however uncritically."

At the midlevel of social development, according to the authors, is Weakley Hollow, beneath Old Rag Mountain, where "agriculture is organized" and "there is a beginning of industry" and the people go to school and church, have a post office, and order goods through mail-order catalogs and "the few people who recognize their limitations but lack the intelligence and vigor to surmount them are able to rationalize themselves into the belief that they are living under ideal conditions."

Nearing the bottom of the scale is Nicholson Hollow, where "a few men are literate" and "occasional religious meetings are conducted" and the "cultivated ground approaches the status of farms."

Finally, "at the lowest level of social development in this region" is Corbin Hollow. They describe how Corbin Hollow has "no community government, no organized religion, little social organization" and that "the ragged children, until 1928, had never seen the flag or heard of the Lord's Prayer." They also state that "the community is almost completely cut off from the current of American life."

"No one in this hollow can read or write. There are no cattle or poultry in the Hollow proper . . . Neither is there a church." In addition, "nearly all the inhabitants are blood relatives."

They do things "dumbly" and are "backward" and "slow."

One woman is referred to as a prostitute. Children are called "neglected urchins."

Reminiscent of Edgar Allen Poe's "A Tale of the Ragged Mountains," which he wrote in the 1840s while a student at the University of Virginia and in which he refers to "strange stories told about these Ragged Hills, and of the uncouth and fierce races of men who tenanted their groves and caverns," "a haunted valley" is how the researchers describe Corbin Hollow.

"At all hours the forms of nature undergo weird transformations in the twilight of the thickets," Sherman and Henry wrote. "The children who hide in the sassafras tangles are gnome-like creatures. The fluttering mountain shadows make ghosts and demons of the dead, white chestnuts, and the bare rocks. One walks over unmarked graves. Towering over all is the highest peak in this section of the mountains whose crest has been carved by countless centuries of winter tempests with the crude outline of a human face"—a mountain we call Stony Man today.

These guys weren't the first to "study" the mountain folk, nor the first to stereotype or make judgment without a cultural yardstick or a sensitivity to the history or migration of various peoples to this country, the traditions and preferences and folkways from their homelands. They weren't the first to not know that the

frequent preference for mountains and temporary structures and an isolationist life of proud self-sufficiency
and self-government was carried overseas in the hearts
of many of the Blue Ridge residents, that their way of
speaking—as with all language nuance—comes from
somewhere culturally, historically, and socially, not necessarily out of ignorance. Upon publication of *Hollow
Folk*, the *Boston Transcript* reported that the book was presented "without bias"; a *New York Times* reviewer called
the Blue Ridge hollows "a leprous spot on our national
body." In 1935 a headline about the nearby park residents
in the *Washington Post*—a newspaper sold, incidentally,
at the Old Rag Post Office store (along with Coca-Cola
and Nehi soda)—read, "Mountain Folk Know Nothing
of Our Age," noting that they "liv[e] in what is probably
the most primitive existence in all the United States."

Alas, when the *Hollow Folk* researchers moved away
from Corbin Hollow to a different area for study and
said that they "have emerged from the backwash of
Time," they were not the first to disparage the mountain ways. Or the last.

Singing the same tune in the same era, a young
woman named Miriam Sizer, a teacher who worked
in the summer of 1928 at a private "vacation school"
in the Old Rag community—one that operated in the
non-school-year months only—drafted a letter she had
planned to send to an editor at *The New York Times* who
was a proponent of the park: "The school has instilled in
the children no sense of citizenship; there is no school
flag; and neither children nor parents, until this summer had ever heard 'America' sung." She sent the correspondence first to Cammerer, who was then the director
of the National Park Service, and was then convinced
not to forward it to the newspaper editor, as he "might
stir up a whole lot of publicity on it."

"These mountaineers have aptly been called 'our contemporary ancestors,'" she wrote. "Steeped in ignorance, wrapped in self-satisfaction and complacency, possessed of little or no ambition . . . little comprehension of law, or respect for law, these people present a problem that demands and challenges the attention of thinking men and women."

"With the acquisition of this territory by the Federal Government," she went on, "these problems will become those of the United States, as well as those of the State of Virginia. Both governments owe it to these people to prepare them as well as possible for the coming change."

Her proposal—to avoid "thrusting out into the world thousands of practically helpless people"—was for Congress to appropriate money to offer elementary and vocational education. Recalling the efforts to save the magnificent American chestnut tree during the early twentieth-century blight that was decimating this species across its entire range, she wrote, "The National Government has expended sums of money to save this valuable national resource. If the Government can spend its wealth to save a race of trees, can it not spend its wealth to save a race of men?"

Later employed by a nebulously benevolent private landowner, George Freeman Pollock, she taught for a year in 1929 at a school serving several Corbin Hollow families, collecting data for what would become *Hollow Folk*. In 1932, when the National Park Service employed her as a collaborator-at-large, or special advisor, to gather sociological information of what were considered the indigent mountain people, she described her Corbin Hollow students as "uncouth" and "a ragged, begrimed, vermin-infested, tobacco-chewing emaciated group."

We also know before entering this place that Pollock— owner of the Skyland resort, a series of cabins he sold to private individuals on his several-thousand-acre parcel of land in prime mountain-vacation country, who had lured Shenandoah National Park to Virginia to promote his lodging business—had used the Corbin Hollow residents to gain support for the park. He had traipsed the posse of potential park supporters through the very path Neil and I are about to take on our hike, in the early stages of park decision making: "I knew that without actually visiting these people in their homes that one could never conceive of their poverty and wretchedness," he said, using their condition as a rationale for proceeding with the park and the people's proposed removal. "I rode next to the Governor telling him tales of Hollow folk."

Some believe Pollock might have actually helped to create their poverty in the first place, luring residents to move to the dark, soil-poor hollow with the promise of work, especially the upper hollow, which had still not been settled by the mid-1800s and was close to Skyland. In fact, he created a sort of company town, staking their untenable futures for his own financial gain and leaving them without a safety net. The work was never regular, sometimes he didn't pay, and the Corbins lived in a feast-or-famine mode for most of their lives (mostly minus the feast).

Whereas in other hollows communities made their living independently—by farming; grazing; selling apples; making legal whiskey; running mills; or harvesting trees for tanbark, nuts, lumber, shingles, barrel staves, or fences—Pollock admitted that "those of Corbin Hollow depended altogether on us for their livelihood," by cutting wood, gardening, and performing construction work for his resort; selling goods such as cookies, white oak–woven baskets, fruit, moonshine, blackberry wine, and huckleberries to Skyland's guests; providing squirrels, chicken, fish, and eggs for preparing guest meals;

building trails; and entertaining the people with exaggerated backward talk and poor-mountain-folk showmanship. The "mountaineers" knew how to put on a show to please the too-dumb-to-know-otherwise city folk.

༄ Neil and I do not normally hike through history in Shenandoah in the summer—it's oppressively hot, as humid as a tropical rainforest, mosquito-y, and, most of all, thickly grown in—but I am too eager to experience the Corbin Hollow I have read so much about to wait until winter.

Everything is different now—the oaks and hickories and tulip poplars have unfurled their slumbering leaves to form a dark umbrella overhead. Some of the poplars are so big that when Neil and I together stretch our arms around their trunks, our span is two feet too short. Witch hazel and Virginia creeper are in profusion, and the invasive multiflora rose has reengaged in battle. All the dry, brown spaces between skeletal branches have been colored in with nature's green Crayola.

We've hiked so many winters in this park and so few summers lately, we feel we are in a foreign land. Instead of a crunchy, barren ground of leaves or needle ice (formed from water that has come to the surface through not-quite-frozen mud in a capillary-type action—excellent to crunch on with a boot), the soil is damp and cast in shadow by everything around it that is alive and growing upward and outward, tickling our legs as we swipe past. Where we do see sky, it is not the icy whiteness of winter but an awning of tremendous blue, dotted with red-eyed vireos and scarlet tanagers, which Neil identifies by sight and sound.

The hike through Corbin Hollow is only two and a half miles from bottom to top, and so we are slow and deliberate about running our eyes over and through the vegetation, lest we miss any artifacts we might spot from the trail. Archaeologists say that the style of architecture was different here, that residents did not build substantial chimneys as in other hollows. Instead of towering stone structures that would remain in the woods, they tended to use loose stone stacks merely to vent woodstoves, and some homes did not use chimneys at all. So we do not know quite what mental image to prepare for what we're looking for.

It is said that Corbin Hollow was one of the narrowest inhabited hollows, that the community was closed in by the mountains, cut off from the outside world, and unable to see beyond the "ghostly trunks of dead chestnuts" or its own squalor or to know there was anything else they could ever want or hope for. But to me, on this first half of trail, the hollow seems wide.

It is also said that this hollow was so rocky that it was impossible to farm, that only the lowliest of people would settle in such a godforsaken place where you could plant no crops and graze no cattle. In the lush greenness of these woods, the damp darkness of the trail, it doesn't seem that this quiet hollow is any more or any less rocky than anywhere else we've been in this park.

You can't believe everything you hear.

~ Jeffrey A. Corbin introduces himself to me over the phone as the great-grandson of "the Corbin who was murdered by a Nicholson."

"It was a murder over moonshine," he explains. Jeff says his great-grandfather allegedly led some revenuers to a still, which they then smashed up. Soon thereafter, he was working in a field. "A man named Nicholson came up on a horse, called my great-grandfather over, and they had a couple words. Then Mr. Nicholson pulled out a revolver and shot him several times, killing him." He was survived by a wife and seventeen children, one of whom was Jeff's grandfather.

Jeff, once a history major, now cross-country truck driver, is the great-great-great-grandson of the first Corbin to settle in the area that would become the park, in 1816, after serving in the War of 1812. He is also the great-great-grandnephew of a man named Finnell Corbin, who in the 1930s was a gray-haired, gray-bearded man with sun-drenched leathery skin, the patriarch at the time of park takeover, whose wife, brother, daughter, son, daughters- and sons-in-law, grandchildren, nephews and nieces, and extended family all surrounded him in Corbin, Weakley, and Nicholson Hollows, true to *Hollow Folk*'s assessment of everyone being related.

Jeff Corbin lives in upstate New York, though he mentions that "by the grace of God, I was born below the Mason-Dixon line." He's been back to Corbin Hollow and nearby Corbin Mountain several times, and he and his sons have stayed in his cousin George T. Corbin's cabin, a refurbished, rentable cabin in the park, operated by the Potomac Appalachian Trail Club. Like many descendants of the pre-Shenandoah mountain residents, he is an avid genealogist who has spent many years researching his family's history, coming to terms with it, and formulating opinions about it.

"*Hollow Folk* was complete fiction," he says. "They portrayed the mountain people as very backwards, very ignorant. It was just propaganda. The government wanted to create empathy and sympathy for them in the general population—everyone feels better when they think they are doing the right thing. To a city dweller, those people living in the mountains must have appeared as cavemen, almost."

Jeff's grandfather was a farmer who worked for Skyland, helping to build things, hauling wood—whatever he was paid to do. Jeff explains that even though it might have been a harsher life than people are used to today, they enjoyed it. "My grandfather would tell me many a time how beautiful the water was, how clear it was. It was a place where if the kids wanted to stay out late at night, they could stay out. It was a tight community; everybody trusted everybody."

"Then it changed very suddenly," he said, when the government began ejecting people, when his grandfather was just in his late teens or early twenties. "My grandfather hated the government after that."

When I asked Jeff if there were any way he could say creating the park was worth it, he was thoughtful and generous in his response. "Was it worth it for the damage that I know it caused to my grandfather and his brother? No. But overall for the complete population of this country that enjoys the park? I guess it was. I try not to look at things one-sided."

When I inquired about how he thought his life would be different if the Corbins never had to leave, he became wistful. "I'd probably be a farmer. Overall, my life would have been a little bit simpler. I kind of would have liked that. An honest day of work. Being paid for it, coming home and raising a family and going to a good church. I think my life would have been very good if we had stayed there."

Not all descendants are as forgiving as Jeff. Elisabeth Weakley, whose paternal grandparents and father were forced off their land, one hollow over in Weakley Hollow beneath Old Rag Mountain, explains that her family—whose ancestors include a Union drummer boy who saw action at Gettysburg as well as conscientious objectors to that war—felt really betrayed by the American government and were particularly unhappy with Miriam Sizer.

"The kinds of things she convinced the American people were going on in those mountains were absolutely false," Weakley says of Sizer. "I really feel aggrieved with the representation of the mountaineers and their families and their lifestyle. Most of them were hardworking people who tended to their farms and took care of their animals and butchered in the fall and ate apple butter and had bees and went to church and sang. They had schools, they were educated, they read the Bibles in their churches. I mean, I don't have a relative who couldn't read and write and do arithmetic. They were decent human beings."

The reputation affected her. "When I was a really little girl, I was reticent to tell people that my family was from the mountains of Virginia because any time I heard people who had no knowledge of the mountaineers and their lifestyle speak, it was always in derogatory terms: 'stupid hillbillies,' 'moonshiners.' I should have known better because I lived with these people and I could see what they were on an everyday basis. But it took me a little while."

Unfortunately, she said, some of her family members "still do suffer a little bit from the poor mountaineers' syndrome."

When asked whether the communities' removal to create the park was worth it, she said, "It's a double-edge sword."

"I do feel kind of happy about the park being there now because otherwise all I could see was a bunch of Swiss-style chalets for rich folks from Washington DC. At least that area that is protected will remain as pristine as possible, and more than just wealthy people will get to enjoy it," presuming the mountain residents might have sold their properties eventually for the right price.

On the other hand, her grandmother and other relatives—as so many of the descendants have reported—

were never the same. She explains that just before her uncle—whose family moved to Pennsylvania after being removed from the park—passed away, "he said to his daughter, 'I want to go home.' She said to him, 'Daddy, you are home.' And he said, 'No, I mean Virginia.' They never got quite over it."

Even in 1929, when the first inflammatory articles by Thomas R. Henry were being published in the *Washington Evening Star*, nearby lowland residents stood by their mountain neighbors. "The first of these articles was read by people of Page County in breathless fashion. They 'knocked the wind out' of the oldest inhabitant," a September 1929 editorial in the *Page News and Courier* read. "There is no class of Ridge people which has never seen the American flag or never heard the Lord's Prayer."

"As a rule, the people living in the proposed Shenandoah National Park are as enlightened, moral, refined and progressive as those living out of the Park," the article continued. "Some of the most prominent and useful citizens of the various counties live in that area. . . . The probable effect of [Henry's] article on the average hasty newspaper reader will be to give a decided impression that he is painting conditions applying to a great many people in the area."

A small cabin site with stove parts and farm equipment gears nearby are the only real indicators we see that someone once lived in this hollow, so five months later, we decide to return to Corbin Hollow. It's Martin Luther King Day this time, and we're in long pants, fleece, gloves, and hats, though it is a rare warm day, punctuating what has been a rather cold, snowy winter. Everything's melted two hours east of the park where we live, and when we arrive at the parking area and trailhead, everything's warm and melted here too. Mountain laurels are green, but the other greenery is gone. We can see right through from one side of the hollow to the other, nothing but the brown deadness in between.

There are patches of snow and ice here and there in this lower section of hollow, and rocks are carpeted in mossy green embroidery. It is indeed quite rocky in the early stretch; perhaps in the summer I didn't notice it quite as much through my eagerness. You have to watch your footing the entire time, as the trail becomes a jumble of ankle breakers. As we climb a bit up into the hollow, I guess I can see why it would be considered narrow—there is, in fact, a wall of mountain on each side. We also notice that Corbin Hollow is unusually cold and dark—the north-facing side never really sees any direct sun, and the south-facing side is always in the shade of Robertson Mountain, an unfortunate fate of the earth's forces for anyone living there.

I start to realize some of the early assessments could have been correct.

Today we come with more data to frame our experience in the times, though. In 1920, for example, fewer than 10 percent of rural homes throughout America had the amenities of electricity, central heating, running water, or indoor toilets, and by 1930 the numbers had only risen to 30 percent. Also in the 1930s, one-fifth of all southern farmhouses had no indoor toilets. In 1940, 98 percent of households in Madison County, Virginia (where part of the park is located), used woodstoves for cooking, not electricity, gas, or kerosene—making those found in the hollows standard even for lowland homes. In 1950 less than half of some of the counties near the park had plumbing. (Even Wayne Baldwin of Bolen Cemetery fame says that when he was growing up in the nearby lowlands, "everyone in the hollow had about the same things: garden, livestock, outhouses.") The fact that homes here in Corbin Hollow, or anywhere in this park, fit these conditions was not so out of the ordinary.

We bring all our maps and gear and some emailed instructions to four cabins sent by my email pen pal, bushwhacker Len Wheat, and we are also accompanied by our bushwhacking buddies, brothers Jeremy and Mike, who have spent their lives poking around in the woods, finding remnants of the past—our backcountry soul mates. Not only do the brothers supply two more sets of eyes, a thirst for the search, and a set of walkie-talkies for us all to stay connected while we each poke around in the woods—"Got something over here," one of us might say to lure the others over to check it out—but they are actually much more curious and patient than either Neil or me; they are more willing to walk aimlessly in unplanned directions without knowing where they might end up.

The water is higher this season in the stream we have to cross, forcing me to confront my stream-crossing phobia. Whether it's a fear of falling in and getting wet or a fear of hurting myself, based on memories from my childhood of splitting my chin open in a bloody mess while running on a log during an obstacle course at camp, I actively avoid hikes requiring major crossings, which has somewhat limited my options in this park.

But I find myself facing Brokenback Run with a strong desire to be on the other side, which means I must cross over on a log. The only way I can will myself across it is by holding on to Neil's back, taking tiny steps, and not looking around too much. Luckily the Ervin brothers—southern gentlemen—are too polite to make fun of my lapse in machismo.

Nearly half of the forest that is now Shenandoah was once towering American chestnut, and the residents who lived here in the chestnut's heyday knew an entirely different forest than we do now. Even the residents who lived at the time of park creation knew a different forest than this: ghost chestnuts littered the landscape; the reign of hemlock, which has since come and gone, had not yet begun; and most of the woods in Corbin Hollow were composed of chestnut oak and red oak. Now the old folks would not recognize where we are. For the four of us, though, it's all we know.

Continuing uphill, we again hit the first cabin site, and with the brush around it gone, I see now that it is truly a tiny cabin, one of the smallest we've seen in the park. I imagine it as in photos I've seen: rough-hewn logs chinked with mud mortar in a kind of cartoonish, somewhat-lopsided Hansel and Gretel cottage, covered over with chestnut bark shingles, which were hardy enough to last fifty or a hundred years. It might be windowless, to keep the heat in more easily, with a shady front porch with wooden stairs, a stone foundation decorated with wildflowers, and weeds growing nearby. It's probably surrounded by a whitewashed picket fence demarking a cleared area around the house, and a handmade wooden ladder would be leaning against an outside wall, for accessing the bark-shingled roof.

Nearby would be a small kitchen garden and woodpiles to heat the house. Here, about seventy-five years later, the area leading up to the cabin is covered with small rock piles and small rock walls—low to the ground with tiny stones and well scattered, nothing massive and carefully stacked like we've seen elsewhere, what many would characterize as a hardscrabble attempt at eking something out of the land in an area with little soil, perhaps.

"We didn't raise too much of nothing because it was so rocky and all," Estelle Nicholson Dodson, one of the former residents of Corbin Hollow, recalled years later. "You had to dig, dig, dig to try to get the dirt to do anything."

She described her house as "just an old shack. We girls slept upstairs, and the snowflakes would come in on us."

With these images in mind, we continue up the hollow, and the trail becomes entirely covered in snow and ice, a dramatic change from the bottom, where we were sweating in full sun and wishing to have not worn so many clothes. The snow is hardened and slick from many weeks on the ground in cold temperatures, but the top layer is melting and slushy, so each step requires twice as much exertion, akin to walking in sand. Each footprint onto or into the slippery mess slips back just a bit. We must walk a bit like penguins, and so combined with stops to satisfy our curiosity, the two and a half miles of the hollow take us nearly all day.

Every so often, we think we see a rock formation, and we either collectively or separately veer off into the woods to investigate. But most of these sightings lead nowhere. Then, just as we are about to descend to cross a small side stream, a few hundred feet above the main stream in the upper hollow, I see a regular shape among irregular shapes, the brown rustiness of a pipe, perhaps, against white snow. Two of them, in fact, nearly side by side. Getting closer, I realize they are not pipes at all, but the two ends of a bed frame curving up at the ends like a sled—a very small bed frame, perhaps for a child.

Looking uphill from here into the slope of snow, Mike notices a defined stone chimney poking out through the snow—a house site! And as we punch our feet through the deeper snow of this north-facing slope, all four of us locate additional objects left behind: a piece of blue-and-white China, a shard of glass, a metal object that's either from a bed spring or part of a cobbler's kit, and a thick leather heel of a shoe ("size 8") with holes where the nails used to be. Though not as big a find as what archaeologists have located throughout this hollow—costume jewelry; toy trucks; porcelain doll fragments, including a Mickey Mouse figurine; a tin ray gun; a baseball; a harmonica; hundreds of fragments of 78-RPM records; an oil lamp made in Czechoslovakia; women's cosmetic bottles; beads and buttons; a muffin tin; and the bottom of a jar of Tabasco sauce—we are thrilled at our find, our sleuthfulness at work.

Although it's nearing dark by this point in our hike and the sun is about to disappear on the other side of the ridge, we've got four eager history hikers with maps who are bent on locating at least one of the three cabins that an online geographic information system (GIS) map says are on the other side of the stream near the top. I join the others and brave crossing the stream one more time to have a look-see—no one's watching me fumble for good stepping stones—and we scramble over rocks to the other bank, where nearly immediately (thanks to Neil's binoculars) we find yet another house site. It is one of the largest house sites we've seen in this park, with a well-stacked stone foundation wall facing the water and a big, well-constructed chimney with extra mortar for fortification, two wash basins, stove parts, a bed frame, and big open pits in the ground for storing vegetables or ice. Based on the historic maps, we believe this is the land and home of Finnell Corbin—Jeff Corbin's great-great-great-uncle—listed by the government as containing a fifteen–by–thirty-four–foot log house with a shingled roof and thirty apple trees.

It has taken us all day to scale this hollow, and once we reach the fire road, on the south-facing slope, everything is still covered with snow. It's at least two more miles back to the car. Now we're on the other side of the ridge, and the same way that daylight savings provides an extra hour to live over again, here we get to see the sun set one more time over the next most westerly ridge and the ragged face of Old Rag Mountain glowing in golden light.

In 1975, forty-three years after initial publication of *Hollow Folk* but just a few years after its republication, Murphy Nicholson, son of the Corbin Hollow woman who was called a prostitute in the book, wrote a letter to the publisher, carbon copied to all nearby national archives, libraries, and relevant federal agencies; to the Virginia governor; and to better business bureaus, denouncing the book, threatening legal action for its continued publication, and recommending that the book not be held by any local institutions. The people so degraded in this book, he said, "lived a simple, uncomplicated life without the cares and worries that beset the current generations. True, they were uneducated. But pray tell me, to what avail is 'high education' if it raises one no higher than to publish literature such as *Hollow Folk*?"

"Our colleges are turning out those who still can't read or write," he wrote. And if the educated city dwellers who wrote and supported the book were so happy and content with their lives, he argued, then why were they turning to "a cute little log cabin in the mountains, where it is quiet, where it is beautiful, where we can unwind, where we can get a breath of unpolluted fresh air, where we can get a drink from a mountain spring."

Of his people, he said, "They knew how to live."

And so it is for the four of us, at least for the day. It's Sunday, the end of a weekend. We trudge the icy fire road until dark and come down the mountain in the light of the silver moon. In our layered fleece, we finish the last of our tea and snacks—our Vermont cheddar cheese and rosemary crackers—and we dig out an old-fashioned glass bottle of original-recipe Coca-Cola that we had buried in the snow at the beginning of our hike as a treat for the end. We notice the flash or two of light from mountain cabins just outside the park boundary, and each of us silently wishes we didn't have to leave this place to find our way home.

ᏋᎦ Stranded

THE NIGHT BEFORE NEIL and I planned to go bush-whack hiking in Shenandoah National Park in December, my mother admonished me over the phone, "You're not going to get stranded anywhere, are you?"

She might have been referring to a weekend two winters ago when we had planned to spend the night at Corbin Cabin, another rehabilitated mountain residence. Snow was expected that Saturday afternoon, a ranger said at the entrance station, and if it started coming down, the park would lock the gates to Skyline Drive and we would be trapped in the park on Sunday. We decided to do a day hike instead, came back up to the car at about 5:30 p.m.—not a flake to behold—drove back to the entrance station, and found the gates locked anyway, in the cold, in the dark, with no explanation other than, we suppose, snow was still predicted sometime during the night.

Or Mom might have been referring to a story I told her about William E. Carson. The story takes place in December 1935, after the government had torched some of the very last houses and evicted some of the last residents by handcuffing and dragging them away. The park had finally become a reality, and Carson was driving to congratulate one of the staff. In an act perhaps of karmic retribution, Carson got trapped in a blizzard on Skyline Drive, his car stuck in a snowdrift overnight. According to one account, "He tried to dig out. There was no traffic, no help. His family, not knowing where he had gone, checked twenty hospitals in the region. Virginia state police, private groups, and detachments from an army depot . . . searched for him. Night came . . . the full personnel of three CCC camps joined the search. Trucks moved in low gear along Skyline Drive with men clinging to the sides peering over the precipices."

In any case, it was a good thing Mom said something about getting stranded, because even though Neil and I are avid hikers, trained in wilderness first aid, experienced in off-trail travel, I might have forgotten that Skyline Drive closes at 5:00 p.m. from November through January.

We had been planning a bushwhack hike for Jeremy and Mike and some of their friends. The brothers had rented two historic cabins near the park boundary and invited thirteen people for the weekend. Neil and I had declined the overnight part of the trip, not wanting to share sleeping space with ten strangers, what with our ear plugs and snoring and other middle-aged baggage, but I selected an area nearby to explore off trail that Len Wheat had recommended. He said that in the vicinity of the ironically named Slaughter Trail, we could find nine cabin skeletons, one cemetery, and a plane crash site, off trail, using abandoned old roads.

We would begin the adventure on top of the mountain, at a trailhead high on Skyline Drive, and work our way down to the sites using cryptic instructions. We had to be back up at the car by 4:30 to get out in time.

The challenge had begun.

In the backcountry, we each have our roles. Neil is a land manager, with a former life as a surveyor and forester. He's methodical. He keeps us level to help us find our targets. Jeremy—endlessly energetic, the younger of the brothers—is a keen old-road-trace finder who is willing to follow any former wagon road to wherever it leads and is particularly interested in old chestnut fence posts and barbed wire. Mike—careful and observant—has a penchant for noting apple trees and any large old tree that might have served as a corner or part of a boundary line or to make shade for cattle amid an open field and for finding historical debris like China shards and shoe leather among the leaf litter.

What I do for these expeditions is prepare.

I'm a map junkie and have pored over the 1929 hand-drawn historical maps that Carson commissioned, which show the names of all the landowners that were displaced for the park and how many acres of farmland and orchards they once owned. I've researched old and new, hard-copy and online U.S. Geological Survey (USGS) topo maps with contour lines showing the ups and downs of elevation, old roads, and decommissioned trails; the modern-day park maps of various decades, with maintained paths; the clues and hints in the history books about how and where people once lived, where they buried their dead, the number and type of buildings on the property. I've noted all the tips from old-timers I've befriended. I cull the likely landmarks, piece together our targets, approximate the distances, map our routes, and set the course for our destinations. I make copies for everyone like a school group leader. I set the search in motion.

For Neil and me, I work on cold-weather clothes and food. For this hike, it's predicted to be in the twenties and windy. I pull out our wool long johns, wool socks, leather hiking boots, fleece layers, down vests, über mittens, and our Nepali wool and fleece hats with ear flaps. Lunch is cheese and crackers, trail mix, chocolate, and fruit, which had always seemed adequate until we met the guys, who outdo us on lunch on nearly every excursion, with egg-and-cheese burritos, full smorgasbords of make-your-own BLTS, or mini camp stoves cooking up hot bean soup.

Then, I gather headlamps, a first-aid kit with an emergency blanket and a GPS beacon, a compass, Swiss Army knife, and water.

Finally, because I can't erase the thought that we could somehow, someway, still get stuck on Skyline Drive on this trip, I toss some survival gear in the back of the car: sleeping bags, a backpacking stove, fuel, and four boxes of mac and cheese.

I call the Skyline Drive–status information line to double-check about the 5:00 closure, make a note to myself to ask the rangers what the emergency get-us-out-of-here phone number is, and set our alarm for 6:00 a.m. in order to meet Jeremy and the gang at the entrance station.

⁀ Being prepared, of course, means that if something should go wrong, you won't even perceive it as having gone wrong because you have everything you need to handle the situation—to avert it or to manage it and move on.

The opposite, of course, is embracing risk.

Winter had just begun in Virginia—quickly, mind you. I had just started to wear my leather jacket every day, my hat and gloves and wool socks, maybe a week before. The basil in the summer garden had only recently turned black from frost. And so it had really never occurred to me—to any of us—that Shenandoah National Park, roughly ninety miles west of home, up to four thousand feet higher in altitude, might *already have snow*, that Skyline Drive, snaking across some of the highest points on the ridge, might *already be closed* due to weather.

We drive two and a half hours from the city to the high country, where colonials and Cape Cods on tenth-of-an-acre lots on land settled in the 1700s give way to townhomes built on old farmland in the 1990s and then to real farms and pastureland and farmhouses, which deliver us to the mountains. (There are three Virginias, someone once told us: West Virginia, northern Virginia near DC, and real Virginia; we enter real Virginia after about an hour.) We notice a light dusting of powder here and there in the high country. As we switchback up Route 33 to the park, rounding the final bend, Neil, who is driving, notes that there is a thin layer of sheer ice on the road just as we approach the park entrance. And once he utters the words, "I bet Skyline Drive is closed," I know the day I had so carefully planned is about to vanish.

Indeed the ranger informs us that we can go no farther on the road.

But I have a plan B in mind. I reach Jeremy on my cell phone and suggest doing the same hike starting from the bottom of the mountain, instead of the top.

When I ask him how many others will be joining us, he says that no one else showed up for the weekend. He and his brother and one dog shared two cabins by themselves.

༺ The next few hours unfold as if we are clowns.

On a narrow dirt road heading to our new starting point among the privately held properties abutting the park in the lowlands, we realize that a key private landowner, whose timber farm property surrounds the beginning of the Slaughter Trail, has adorned his fences, shrubbery, and outbuildings with No Trespassing signs.

There is no parking allowed on either side of the state road, and thus we can't get quick access to the trail.

We park a mile away. The old-timer's instructions say we can begin the mission by hiking an old four-wheeler route on someone else's private land, a quarter mile hike to the park boundary, then side-hill bush-whack our way back to the Slaughter Trail. Neil is ada-mantly opposed to trespassing, and I agree with him in theory. But when Jeremy and Mike point out that if we take another nearby park trail to get up into the park in a roundabout way, we will have to ford a rather large stream, I follow the brothers as if hypnotized, as I will do anything to avoid a river crossing.

Three of us decide to make the illegal passage, while Neil stays on the up-and-up. Soon, though, a smoking chimney at the crest of a hill and the snarls of dogs have us scurrying back down like cockroaches, to catch up with Neil, who at fifty-two is the oldest in our group and clearly the wisest.

We spend the next half hour en route to the park, wending our way a mile up a private road, which is lined with all varieties of tired residences and is so badly marked for hikers that we question ourselves the entire time whether this is the way to the proper trail.

We look at maps. We debate where to cross the river. We thrash through woods on the river's edge for a good long time, scouting for decent stepping-stones, as none of us wants to take our boots off and get wet, or *not* take our boots off and get wet. We finally pick a spot, where the four of us make graceful jetés from one boulder to the next, and then the men spend a half hour building a makeshift bridge out of logs so that Callie the dog will stop shaking and come to the other side. Half the day has disappeared already, so we discuss whether we'll bushwhack up and over the extremely large and steep mountain to our original target, which now seems quite distant, or whether we'll stick to the new trail we've happened on, which is not in our plans, and see what we find in our spontaneity.

The sky is clear but gray. It is cold, but there is no wind. The sun is low enough to plunge us entirely in the mountain shade. We are not uncomfortable, not suffering, and we have nowhere else to be.

But the bubble has burst. No one is pushing for the bushwhack up the mountain to the Slaughter Trail anymore, where all the plans had led, where all the goods were waiting to be found. We mumble halfhearted proposals of what to do from here. We shrug our shoulders. We look at each other, and we look away, our interior conversations—about fear, fatigue, risk, and reward—never making their way out. I don't know whether the three of them see me as the leader or as the weakest link, but I know they'd do whatever I advocated for. And yet I cannot recover my verve for the outing, aimlessly rescouting a new route to where we wanted to begin in the first place.

I have lost my grounding, trust, and faith in the chase, our only anchor.

We stand stationary on the trail, stuck in indecision, moment by moment deadening the adrenaline rush in all of us: we who have never asked questions and who have successfully stormed mountains, methodically plying the secrets of the park for years in the past, finding the unfindable old wagon roads the former residents once used, the hundred-year-old daffodils planted at front stoops, the bed frames, jalopies, root cellars, and tombstones deep in the nothingness, in the empty places of the map that we have charted.

Heading back across the river, my graceful jeté goes haywire when I miss the ideal landing spot on the boulder I'm aiming for, and I hit a slippery slime of moss, which sends me thundering down on a granite face with one foot dangling in the rushing water, fruitlessly trying to find a foothold so I can boost myself up and out. Neil grabs the scruff of my pants to give me a lift. Jeremy quietly remarks that he wishes he had a video camera, and Mike is already heading back to a wide, shallow area upriver where he decides he's willing to take off his shoes and endure the icy water. I limp my soggy, sorry way to shore, and as we resume our walk, I can feel the spread of black and blue under the surface of my stinging calf, which, amazingly, is the only place on my oafish body that has taken a beating.

It's 4:00—one more hour until darkness—and we're heading back to the car with plenty of time to spare. We don't say, *How did our grand hike fizzle into nothing?* We don't utter, *We drove all this way for this?* I'm guessing Mike never expected a demanding hike. Jeremy is content with whatever unfolds in the universe. Neil is wishing we'd have spent more time *somewhere* to take in the essence of the landscape. I'm regretting we didn't spend the night with these good guys in their empty extra cabin, cooking over a fire in sooty pots and playing games by candlelight, instead of being homebodies with hang-ups. I'm also wishing that we could have at least had a shot of getting locked in on the drive today: something, anything, I could not control.

Back at the cars, we shake hands, pat backs, and hug goodbye: we four friends who gather only here, in this park, on cold days, to meet the mountain. Out here, where life is real, we are stripped bare of whoever we are in the rest of the world. Neither of the duos knows the other any other way but muddy and sweaty, in the backwoods, discovering other people's buried past and negotiating the undulating terrain of our individual psyches.

There's a story and there's no story in our journey of stranding ourselves, in the heart of this sacred and ordinary place, and I find myself thinking about what the writer Annie Dillard once said: "How we spend our days is, of course, how we spend our lives." There's not much to say here at the end of this day, and so we don't speak it. But as the gravel shoots out the back wheels and our two vehicles begin the long slog back to civilization, with the hazy Blue Ridge at our backs, I know the only thing coursing through each of our minds now is: *Next time.*

⟲ The Trespass

WE KNOW FROM THE beginning that this hike could wind up being illegal.

My 1988 park map shows this path as being a "dry weather or private road," and my 2007 map shows just a tiny bit of road near a gate that terminates into nothingness within a few hundred feet. Later we'll acquire an old USGS map showing a bona fide trail. But for now, I know from my online research, from one of dozens of genealogical sites where Blue Ridge descendants converge, that this is the route to the Via family cemetery.

The route begins on a wide and well-worn path of straw-colored grass and a virtual fence of vegetation on each side. Where the trail heads downhill to the left, we take a footpath to the right. It's narrow and, though the bushes have been trimmed back to allow passage, it doesn't look like it gets much regular use. There are no signs or blazes installed by the National Park Service; no cement posts at trail junctions or colored strips painted on trees. But after a few minutes, we see the first clue that we're headed in the right direction: a fluorescent-orange spray-painted *V* on a log. In fact, from that point forward, the entire trail is lined with live trees and downed logs that are either spray painted or carved with *V*s. We can only assume this paint job was performed by a member of the Via family to help point relatives in the right direction.

We are on national park land at this point, though,

and spray painting park trees is probably an unlawful act. I know that descendants of the people who once lived on these lands before the government turned it into a park can obtain keys that allow them to drive on roads otherwise closed to the public to access their ancestors' cemeteries. They are allowed to bring in tools and conduct maintenance within cemeteries that are not located on wilderness lands. The park waives fees for descendants visiting their people underground. Perhaps looking the other way on the rather innocuous spray painting on a trail that's no longer on the current park maps is another tiny concession the park has made to park orphans.

Within half a mile, we pass a beat-up, hand-carved wooden sign for the Via Family Cemetery, and the trail changes nearly imperceptibly. The walking surface is still narrow—only as wide as our two feet—but we are actually engulfed in a deep rut that was once a road. Most of the road bed—once five or six feet wide or more—is now filled in with mountain laurels, a profusion of green in what would otherwise be a woodlot of thin, brown, leafless sticks, so thick they seem to grow back together to fill in the trail once we pass through. While I admire this road that once was, my husband Neil—ever the naturalist—takes photos of the many piles of old, dried bear scat we are finding, for his Facebook page called Name That Scat.

If this is the route that present-day Via family members must take to the cemetery, I am concerned. Quite a few trees have fallen over this trail, so we must climb over or under them, and the mountain laurel around us is too thick to take an alternate route. I cannot imagine that the elderly relatives would ever be able to get here if they wanted to, a complaint I have heard from descendants from all over the park who are eager to access their family cemeteries now encased in wildness.

Keeping our eye out for the Vs—sometimes just small

faded notations that are hard to see on dark trunks—we find the laurel-enclosed trail opening up onto a big, flat area with scant vegetation on both sides: hardly a bush, hardly a tree to be found, just ropy vines hanging onto skeletal woody remains. We surmise that this area was probably used at one time for apple orchards or farming. Neil suspects that after the trees were initially cleared for human use, they grew back, then were destroyed again by gypsy moths—insects that were brought to the United States in the late 1800s for starting a silkworm industry but that wound up becoming invasive pests, ravaging the foliage of trees and destroying entire forests. Views in both directions are barren and trashy looking now, here in the flat leading into Via Gap.

But we're not taking this hike for the scenery, like most of the excursions we took in the early years of hiking this park. Used to be, we'd pick a location for the view or the type of landscape we'd traverse—White Oak Canyon for the swimming holes; Old Rag for the climb; Hazel Mountain country for the undulating hills, waterfall, and cave. Now we choose nearly all our hiking routes based on the history they contain. This one has no views in either direction, no balds, no peaks, no visual respite, just a second- or third-growth landscape that reflects the past and yet has been left alone to grow toward the future—a place not curated for beauty.

This hike is an anomaly all around. It is not a bushwhack hike per se, and it's not exactly a park-maintained trail. It doesn't even lead anywhere that the park—or anyone else—wants us to go. It's less than two miles long, and at the end, we'll find ourselves at the U.S. Department of the Interior–National Park Service boundary line, deadended at a landlocked piece of private ground. But the journey over this country symbolizes to me—beyond anything else—the people's fight to keep their land.

By the time a man named Robert H. Via hit the create-Shenandoah-National-Park-by-displacing-the-residents scene in 1934, thousands of people and big landowners like timber companies had already left the mountains. Those who remained included the ones who said they'd never leave no matter how much they were paid, the ones who argued that the sale value of their lands would not be enough to remain self-sufficient somewhere else, and those who simply had nowhere else to go.

The road Robert H. Via would take to the halls of justice was paved by another landowner, however. Thomas J. Rudacille, owner of 685 acres and a descendant of Swiss pioneers who settled in the area two centuries earlier, decided he would file suit against the commonwealth, first in Warren County Circuit Court in 1929 and later with the Supreme Court of Appeals of Virginia in 1931. Among other complaints, he argued that notifying citizens of taking the land by posting announcements in newspapers they don't read or in public places like courthouses that they don't visit (using legal descriptions of properties like "Thence S. 60° 35' E. 1978 ft. to Pos. No. 518") was not adequate notification and that a park was not a necessity for the public good and thus was not just cause for constitutional taking.

A small group representing about twenty thousand acres of land, the Landowners Protective Association, started by landowner Lewis Willis, supported Rudacille and the claim of unconstitutional ejection of residents. Willis—descendant of British gentry, graduate of the University of Virginia, owner of 229 acres with 50 acres of prime bluegrass pasture—wrote to President Hoover, saying, "We are willing to make any reasonable sacrifice for the public good when necessary. We are unwilling to part with our homes to advertise a few politicians and to help a small part of our population get their hands into tourists' pockets."

To engage other landowners, he wrote in a local newspaper, "Landowners are informed that it will be in their interest to keep quiet—not to get in the way of the steam roller. Is it possible in this vaunted land of liberty that a citizen is afraid to protect his constitutional rights? Woe, woe, unto the people of the world when the goddess of liberty becomes an emblem of oppression."

One member of the group, Melanchton Cliser—owner of forty-six acres on a major thoroughfare, where he and his wife operated a gas station, store, and lunchroom and kept a two-story, seven-room home that his father built, with two chimneys, an indoor bathroom, indoor plumbing, and electricity—said his piece as well. "The fundamental principles of our government are to protect those who can't protect themselves, and to restrain the rich and the strong from oppressing the poor and the weak," he wrote in an editorial in a local paper in October 1929. "And only eternal damnation awaits any party that gets away from the sound doctrine laid down by our forefathers generations ago."

Aside from this one group and these three fiery individuals, however, the communities didn't really organize to save their land from the government, as many communities would do today. Could be because residents were never fully informed of the park's plans and were often only alerted after all the major decision making had taken place—no public meetings, stakeholder involvement, formal resettlement assessment plans, or mediation here. Could be because residents didn't know what their options were in terms of using the law to their advantage. Could be because they were too geographically isolated from one another to meet in person and organize—communities in the north were nearly one hundred miles away from those in the south, and "often a mere cross ridge dividing hollows in the same county is as much a barrier between small mountain settlements as if the distance were a thousand miles and the dividing ridge an ocean," as one astute official wrote.

Could be because the lowland farmers who used their upland pastures only from April until October for grazing cattle—nonresident landowners—were in a different position than the mountain residents who had nowhere else to go. It wasn't that the lowland ranchers weren't angry. "If somebody had shot . . . Will Carson, Pollock, and Hoover, there'd never have been a park" is what one son of a lowland rancher-landowner is recorded as saying; another, imploring President and Mrs. Roosevelt later in 1933 and 1934 to do something about the impending resident evictions, said, "It will virtually destroy my little cattle business, to take my grazing land away; and not give me enough to secure other grazing land in its place." But they might not have hired lawyers, some surmise, because there was general economic hardship in the region and they needed the state's money to keep their more valuable lowland farms secure.

Could be because so many of the mountain residents considered themselves to be patriotic, law-abiding, tax-paying, landowning citizens who believed in their government—these were people who had fought in the Revolutionary War, the War of 1812, and the Civil War. "It was beyond comprehension to fight the government," sisters and descendants Ruth Kiger and Jean Morris said of their forefathers, who had fought in those wars and owned and lost their land. "The mountain people didn't resist. They had faith. They didn't believe in protest. They believed in their government, and they did not believe in calling attention to themselves."

Robert H. Via did not feel the same compunction. He decided to follow in Rudacille's pioneering footsteps and bring another case to court.

꙼ The temperature is probably in the forties, and we've stripped off a few layers of fleece by the time we reach the property line—marked by one "Private Property No Trespassing" sign and a barbed wire fence that's clearly been stepped over numerous times. A downy woodpecker greets us at this spot. An orange spray-painted *V* on the same tree on which the No Trespassing sign is posted points us to the left. Our online directions—written by a Via family member who requests that the "hallowed grounds of my Great-Great Grandfather Christopher and many of our ancestors" be tread on softly—indicates that the "Via Cemetery will be there on your left." But it is not.

Before us is a patch of leafless trees in a wood, thick enough that we can't see through to the other side. We are guided by a dirt road with tire tracks that follows the fence line to the left, with scraggly trees on both sides. We don't know who exactly owns this property now, whether it is in use, whether it's hunting season, whether we're at risk, where we're going, or what we might find, so we skulk along the fence rather haltingly. I have what I consider permission to be here: a series of printouts from a great-great-granddaughter of Robert H. Via, with whom I struck up a brief email conversation a few months ago, wherein she says, "I think this private land is partly mine," and I tell her I am planning to go there and she does not object.

We work our way along the fence and hit a corner that we are expecting based on the shape of the property line on our map. We then find ourselves officially in Via Gap, heading toward Cedar Mountain, a trailless hump of a peak on park land. Once in a while, we get a glimpse of what's behind the veneer of woods: a freshly brush-hogged strip, clear and wide as a highway.

I'm unsure about continuing ahead, as I've never trespassed before. I don't know what the consequences are. Could we get arrested? Go to jail? I am not even related to these people, for God's sake. But the history of the Blue Ridge families draws me here.

Though my own family tree is truncated—I don't know much about any generation beyond my grandparents—this place and this history is something I can know, research, travel through, and adopt. The family trees here are full and far reaching; people know each branch and each twig from two centuries or more ago. Maybe the attachment I feel here for the older folks long gone and the culture erased is a proxy for what I'll never know about my own people and land we never owned. Because I walk their land and sit in the skeletons of their homes and take pleasure in the jonquils they planted long ago, I mourn their passing, in a sense, as if they were my own blood.

Neil—the patient one—pushes against my reticence and encourages us onward, and soon we see a fenced plot on the edge of the brush-hogged path. We also see a small roofed structure nearby, which we assume is a deer blind. We must emerge from the woods in full sight of whoever might be watching and walk past the blind into the clearing to enter the burial ground through the front gate.

Gently, with reverence, in the blazing sun of a winter morning, we find the gate unlocked and open the door to the past.

Robert H. Via was a robust six-foot-three-inch, 250-pound man, known throughout the area where he hauled in sugar to make brandy and whiskey as the "King of

Sugar Hollow." A shrewd and efficient manager, he was also a man who is said to have asked anyone who walked by his home in the morning, "Have you had your breakfast yet?" and offered some of whatever was being made.

"If you're my friend, what I have belongs to you," is what one neighbor of Robert H. Via said of Via's and other mountain residents' approach to life. "This is the way they lived."

He ran his apple business in the Blue Ridge, spending five months a year on the 152-acre mountain tract with his orchards and the rest of the year in Pennsylvania. He wasn't poor, he wasn't a tenant or squatter, he didn't earn his living by doing backbreaking work with his hands, and he didn't share the belief that "whatever will be will be" that many of the residents are reported to have had, such was their deep faith in God.

But like many of the other people here in the Blue Ridge and elsewhere in the Appalachians, he felt tied to his land. For these rural southerners, the land is the root of the family. "You always have a home if you have the land," descendant Ruth Kiger told me her mother once said, remembering the apples, nuts, and other cash crops the family land once provided. "And when you lose the land, you lose everything."

Robert Via was the great-great-great-great-great-grandson (or seven generations removed) of the first Via known to have come to Virginia, a French Huguenot who fled his country to escape religious persecution and a certain death. At the time of park condemnation, Robert was the sixth generation of Vias to have inhabited the Blue Ridge and likely the fourth to carry on the family's apple business.

Robert's father, Christopher Columbus Via, and his mother met in the Blue Ridge. They built their home on what they called Via Mountain and nurtured a huge apple orchard: lower grades for brandy and Albemarle pippins for fruit—the most prized of American dessert apples in their heyday in the 1700s and 1800s. Grown most ideally in Albemarle County, Virginia, and sold as far away as England, where they were consumed by the queen, Albemarle pippins were planted widely by men like George Washington and Thomas Jefferson. Orchard owners describe them as "hard as bullets until February" and say they ship well. The Vias employed at least a dozen laborers and used mountain roads through the gaps to move apples off Via Mountain.

Business must have been going well. The Vias' nine-room, two-story home had hand-carved chestnut wood interiors, a Victorian oak banister leading from the 576-square-foot living room to the bedrooms on the second floor, a 648-square-foot kitchen, a dining room, and a wraparound porch. One orchard worker called it a mansion. They kept a tool house, two garages, a barn, a smoke house, a hen house, a packing house, a cellar house, another house, and a small five-room dwelling.

The main house was where Robert grew up. Mother kept a garden and some cows, canned, labeled apple barrels for shipping, and fed the workforce and fifteen children from the fruits of her labors. This is the life he lived as part of a hardworking but well-rewarded mountain family. And this is the business he inherited in 1906 at age twenty-four when his father died; he continued the family's work, planting two thousand more trees, running the orchard as well as overseeing farming, livestock raising, and timbering operations with the help of tenants. He needed help with the physical labor, because he couldn't do much work himself; in 1901 he had burned his hands in a brush fire, trying to save his sister Rosie—his father's darling—leaving his digits painful and gnarled.

Several decades before talk of a park began, he had already demonstrated he was willing to risk it all for what he loved.

On December 14, 1933, after the state had assessed all of Robert H. Via's land and structures—appraisers had counted 983 apple trees, six cherry trees, nine quince trees, eight peach trees, four Damson plum trees, and seven pear trees, all noted to be thirty years old and in poor condition, with the other thousand trees dead or dying from the massive 1930 drought—the Commonwealth of Virginia issued him a check for $3,230 ($55,600 in 2013) for his 152-acre lot, thus officially taking the Via property and apple business.

On November 10, 1934, Robert H. Via, age fifty-one, filed suit in the U.S. District Court for the Western District of Virginia in Harrisonburg, Virginia, arguing that the state buying land to donate to the federal government did not fit the definition of "the public good" and would not fill a need of the residents of Virginia. He stated that the procedure for the condemnation of these lands (to condemn at once all the lands in each of eight counties rather than individual negotiations) constituted arbitrary discrimination against the owners of the Blue Ridge Mountain lands and that he was not given adequate notice before condemnation proceedings began.

He also filed suit in the District of Columbia Supreme Court to try to prevent the U.S. secretary of the interior from accepting the deeds for the park from the Commonwealth of Virginia, because Via claimed that his orchards—Albemarle pippins—as well as his valuable timber plots and grazing land were worth $15,000 ($260,900 in 2013), not the lesser amount he was assessed.

Above all, in *Via v. State Commission on Conservation and Development of the State of Virginia*, he argued that the state had violated his Constitutional rights—in particular, the Fifth Amendment "Takings Clause," which states that "Private property shall not be taken for a public use, without just compensation," and the Fourteenth Amendment, which states that "No State shall make or enforce any law which shall abridge the privileges or immunities of citizens of the United States; nor shall any State deprive any person of life, liberty, or property, without due process of law; nor deny to any person within its jurisdiction the equal protection of the laws."

The lawyer for the Commonwealth of Virginia was William E. Carson's brother, the man whose idea it was to utilize a blanket condemnation in the first place, and the majority opinion in the case was written by a judge who had served as the regional fundraising chairman when the idea of Shenandoah National Park was just a twinkle in the park-for-profit-minded businessmen's eyes. But no one seemed concerned about the conflicts of interest.

On January 15, 1935, the three-judge panel ruled against Via. Among their findings, disagreeing with all of Via's points, the judges determined that happiness, health, and pleasure are a public purpose for which a state can indeed use eminent domain.

Aside from appealing to God, Via had only one more place to plead his cause: the highest court in the land.

The cemetery is large—about fifty feet by twenty-five feet—and at first glance, I would estimate two dozen visible graves. The sun casts long shadows to the east, toward the park, and we are looking straight ahead to the boundary line, red-tipped posts of the National Park Service draped with dead weeds and vines.

Someone has cleared this plot recently; there are no leaves, no branches or sticks, no long dead grasses. Small tree trunks have been sawed off at ground level. The land inside the fence undulates like an ocean wave, giving the place a sense of movement, as though things have not always been this way here and they will continue to evolve. The sunken areas are, of course, places where the ground has caved in due to decay, the rot of wooden boxes, the natural decomposition of flesh: tiny microorganisms performing nature's services.

The markers themselves also appear to be in motion, no longer standing perfectly upright, no longer parallel to one another, as a field of granite headstones would stand in a modern cemetery. Like crooked teeth in a mouth, some lean forward, some lean back, some have fallen over completely, some are broken. The scene is cartoonlike in its haphazardness, yet serene and lovely nevertheless.

Some of the stones are marble, professionally carved; others are fieldstones, unmarked or labeled with a small, rectangular metal plaque. They are headstones and footstones, rectangular, squared off, or rounded at the top.

There are only two obelisks in the graveyard. One belongs to Rossie L. Viare (Rosie Via), born May 29, 1890, died April 6, 1901, age eleven. The second is her father, the patriarch of this clan, the last of the Virginia Vias: C. C. Viar, who is (again, despite someone's alternative spelling) Robert H. Via's father—Christopher Columbus Via, born June 22, 1860, died May 9, 1906, five years after his beloved daughter perished. (Former neighbor Raymond P. Wood once postulated that, "like the English did back in the seventeenth century, [people] wrote like the word sounded.")

Six other Vias and Viares, buried from 1881 to 1940, surround father and daughter.

We visit each grave. We try to make out the writing. The sky is a tremendous blue and clear. No one is hunting. We do not see a soul. We do not know if anyone is watching us.

Our online instructions urge us on, but we are afraid to continue to the apple orchard and the old crumbling stone foundation and chimney of Christopher Columbus Via's homestead. Even the author of these directions does not recommend going farther than the Via School unless we're on bikes, as it is two more miles away. So we content ourselves with examining the hunting shelter. We cross the wide expanse of mowed land for a fuller view of the landscape, and we wonder what providence saw fit to exempt this particular piece of land from park property, hemmed in on three sides as it is by government land.

One expects great fanfare when a case is brought to the U.S. Supreme Court: in-depth questioning from the justices, weeks or months of debate, a dramatic oral argument, groundbreaking and contentious or academically significant decisions, a case to go down in the record books, the stuff that movies are made of.

None of that happened when Via appealed his case there.

On November 25, 1935, this court—the same entity that in 2005 would affirm a lower court ruling in *Kelo vs. City of New London* that broadened the definition of the "public good" in eminent domain cases to such extremes that it OK'd taking private property from individual homeowners and delivering it to a multinational pharmaceutical company to enable economic development and expansion of a town's tax base, a decision that so alarmed states that forty-four of them passed laws aimed at curbing the abuse of eminent domain for private use—simply affirmed the U.S. District Court's ruling against Via.

Case closed.

For the park planners, this case—which had held up the park for years—allowed park arrangements to move forward, allowed it to open to the public, to welcome the throngs who came to see the misty blue ridges, the waterfalls, and the wildlife, just as they had been promised.

For Via, it was a sign to move on. In honorable defeat, he moved to Pennsylvania permanently, rebuilt his fortune on a hog and dairy farm, and, out of principle, never cashed the check from the government for his land. While some of the most influential park planners wound up having heart attacks, dying early, and suffering demotions in rank and other misfortunes after the park opened, Via lived comfortably on a large property in the Keystone State into his late eighties. Perhaps he knew intuitively that the best revenge is living well.

As for our foray back in time, Neil and I would find out eventually that the private Via cemetery land on which we are trespassing was owned at the time of park creation by a man named Thomas J. Wood—not, as we had expected, by one of the Vias. It is currently owned by the White Hall Hunt Club and off-limits to nonmembers due to liability rules. Why is the Via family cemetery on Wood land? The law books show me the answer.

In an old deed book in the Circuit Court of Albemarle County is a record on delicate yellow pages. In a handwritten ledger, it is noted that Christopher Columbus Via, Robert's father, left this plot of land to some of Robert's siblings and other relatives (Robert's inheritance lay to the south). They, in turn, sold it to Wood, anathema to the great fight to save Via land.

But they held on tight to their heritage despite the sale; while the family sold the 112 acres to the Woods—boundaries described in old-fashioned metes and bounds with terms like "10 poles past grave-yard" and "23 poles to red oak, S 13 W 25 poles to a stump 3 chops on top," they exempted one acre, containing the graveyard, where they reserved a right-of-way "across and over the land hereby conveyed to and from said grave yard, for themselves and others who may bury within."

As Virginia law states that the right of families to access cemeteries, once reserved, remains indefinitely, perhaps in the end my sort-of permission to be on this land from a printed-out email from a fourth-generation Via descendant, who had never seen or set foot on the land but nevertheless is related to Robert H. Via and the graveyard residents by blood and whose aunt still possesses the government's check that Via never cashed, was legitimate after all.

Lost and Found in Shiflet Country

THE SNOWS IN VIRGINIA had reached four feet deep. I had switched from hiking in the mountains two hours from my house to cross-country skiing and snowshoeing on the bike trail in the county park a few ski lengths from my front door. As an office worker who had never been a superexerciser, I had transformed from a weekend warrior to an everyday outdoor enthusiast in the two weeks of this winter storm. My road was impassible. The federal government—just ten minutes away in Washington DC—was closed. Schools were closed, and so my husband, a teacher, was home. I was enjoying the fact that I had left my job two months earlier to start a new life as a full-time writer.

Then the snow began to melt. The streets were plowed, and so cars and buses were moving again. The schools opened, and so my husband went to work again. I went back to the computer screen.

But everything had changed.

I woke up one morning with a pulsing headache so intense it took my breath away; the next, with an icy-hot feeling on my left side. I became drenched with fatigue, deprived of nearly all my strength on one side. After an MRI, a CT scan, a spinal tap, and two visits to the ER, I was diagnosed with transverse myelitis, a neurological disorder, and I worried about working again, about driving, and about growing old. But above all else, I worried that I'd never be able to hike. The mountains where Neil and I had spent so much time over the past twenty years were so far away, and so uphill. Walking around the house and up the stairs had become such a very slow and deliberate process and quite precarious, due to my poor balance, coordination, and strength. I could not stand up in the shower and lather my hair at the same time or balance on one leg when putting on pants. The notion that I might never get out in the woods again for the fresh, clean air; for the wide open space; for the cemeteries hidden in the woods, which had become my life's fascination, was very real indeed and had quite unhinged me.

But like the snowy-city shutdown, I recovered. After eight weeks of drug treatment and rest and physical therapy and slow, ten-minute walks, I regained everything that I had lost, and the first thing I wanted to do, once I got my functioning back, was find my way through the woods. For my first journey out after a long hiatus, on the first day of spring, my husband Neil and I picked an off-trail area of the park we'd never been to. I call it "Shiflet Country."

The Shiflets are a long line in Virginia, and many consider this area of Shenandoah National Park to be the epicenter of their family's Blue Ridge heritage, when they—along with thousands of other families—made their homes in the mountains, as early as the 1700s or 1800s, as European settlers. When the Commonwealth of Virginia began conducting land surveys and making assessments of the land in that area in the 1920s and 1930s, surveyors noted about one hundred Shiflet, Shiflett, Shifflet, and Shifflett landowners in two counties.

I wanted to come to Shiflet Country because I'd never bushwhacked the old roads there, had never seen the stone foundations and the daffodils that still emerge from a hundred years ago, and because I wanted to see the geography where one particular patriarch, and one particular son, once lived. The older man was Ambrose Shifflett, long gone, and his son is Kenneth Shifflet. And in 1935, in the final days of a couple of centuries of proud self-sufficiency, after months of official warnings and eviction notices, yet just one day before this Shifflet family had planned to remove their belongings and vacate their home to make way for the national park, the government had burned their house to the ground.

We pick an off-trail backcountry hike recommended by Leonard Wheat to a Shiflet cemetery and farm site just north of Bacon Hollow and Shiflets Hollow and east of Beldor Hollow, private areas spared by the park where Shiflets still live. On the park map, amid parallel contour lines indicating the rise and fall of land, a low spot between two small mountains forms a saddle, or gap. It is here, Wheat tells me, that we will find the hidden past.

And so, after several weeks of isolation due to the paralyzing amounts of snow and then my homebound convalescence, we head out on my rehabilitation hike—to test my legs and teach them to walk off trail on uneven ground again, to claim some small piece of history that, for others, would never be recovered.

⌒ We begin on the Appalachian Trail, just a tiny segment of the 2,178-mile footpath that wends its way from Maine to Georgia. We are on this gloriously flat, smooth, well-blazed, and well-maintained trail for less than ten minutes when we decide it's time to heed the instructions Wheat had emailed to me and turn off into the brush.

The directions he's provided were written five years ago, so when he says that the side road we are to turn off onto is "indistinct at first," he has quite understated this fact. We have accurately found the level area of the Appalachian Trail that he describes at the point of the turnoff, but the seven-foot wall of fuzzy, brownish-reddish raspberry brambles make plunging through the woods as appealing as diving into a bed of nails. We vow to wear leather work gloves next time to help in moving barbed branches away from our bodies. For now, we search for the least dense area to contend with and begin slithering our way between barbed obstacles, like a constant sideways limbo in an Amazon jungle full of thorn-studded monkey-no-climb.

I am completely dependent on Neil to navigate us here, as he feels confident about how to get us around Roundtop and through to the valley that meets the bottom of Bush Mountain, even without the old road to guide us, and I have no sense of it. A small round circle on the map, the apex of a knoll, where a contour line comes back around and meets itself, is our beacon. In my post-illness weakened state, I need to concentrate on not tripping or stumbling and do not have the mental capacity to worry about navigation. Neil does not even need a compass to lead the way; he is able to see how land moves and what lies ahead as if there are no trees or other obstructions, as if he has a GPS-connected aerial map plugged into his brain.

Despite my confidence in Neil, however, I do what I always do when we're plunging through the trailless areas of the backcountry on our own: I doubt. I assume we are lost and lose patience and feel as though finding where we're going is impossible and the day is hopeless. We hike for about twenty minutes in the direction that the old road ought to go, according to logic and to Wheat, walking while untangling ourselves from the thumbtack points of greenbrier and raspberry thorns and a maze of dead brownness that is the forest around us. We are always scanning the ground for some kind of giveaway, a telltale sign—a rut, a too-conveniently-neat pile of rocks. We keep the Appalachian Trail to our back, so at least, I think to myself, we will know how to get out of here when it comes time to abandon the mission.

Of course, we finally come to the old road. It is as distinct—or as indistinct—as any grown-over old road in this park, an indented trace in the ground covered over in leaves. Though we are in a narrow section of park that is actually only about two miles wide and surrounded by private farmland with occasional homes on either side, civilization seems very far away from here.

The information Wheat provided is an enigma. Each deliberate line of text must be deciphered like a code. He says that within about one hundred feet from where we were to turn off on this road, which was invisible to us at the time, we should have seen animal paths, two large trees, a white piece of sheet metal, a well, a house foundation, a stone wall, a pail, and a tub. We have bypassed it all. As we walk, we never find the right-hand fork he says makes a beeline to the cemetery. Instead we find ourselves going southwest, away from the knoll we're seeking. We have with us a description of the cemetery from the first employee of the park when it opened in 1936—when these woods were farms, with easy, overland access—and he warns that the cemetery we're searching for is "quite far down."

When we have descended down far enough in the wrong direction, Neil suggests we leave the road and head out through the woods for some pure bushwhacking—unassisted by any book or remnant of man, going with gut instinct and intuition and judgment, the winging-it approach that usually leads us to where we want to go but is like being a cartoon character suspended in air, waiting to fall, until we get there. I can see the mountains whose valley we are headed for, and so I muster up my faith. I follow Neil like a dutiful wife. We are looking for boxwoods, those nonnative, evergreen, ornamental plants much loved in Virginia and much detested by Neil, who is repelled and repulsed by their cat-pee scent, stronger than a week-old litter box. Wheat says we will see two of them near the knoll, marking the cemetery grounds.

After another twenty minutes of walking through the woods—fairly open with easy passage here, coming across the correct old dirt road again, lined with rocks on one side, wide and quite unobstructed in some places, giving me an easier time of imagining it in its horse-and-wagon or Model-T heyday—we feel we are in the vicinity of the dead. The underbrush has thinned, and the sky is bright. I am very happy to be here, wherever we are, and to be well, leg moving in front of leg, in the woods, in the past, in the mountains, with my husband, who has tended to me and cared for me and watered me back to life. I walk with E. E. Cummings, chanting silently:

> i thank You God for most this amazing
> day:for the leaping greenly spirits of trees
> and a blue true dream of sky;and for everything
> which is natural which is infinite which is yes

But my right leg is tired. The mile or so we've walked is more exercise than I've gotten for two months—legs lifting above rock, legs lifting above log—and I wait for Neil to make the call about where to go from here. He stands up on a downed log, like an explorer on a mountain searching for a distant shore, and with his binoculars—brought along today in hopes of catching some of the first neotropical migratory birds of spring—he can see, through the tall, straight regenerated forest in what once was no doubt a field, two mammoth green bushes in the distance: the boxwoods. Hobbling, with my log of a walking stick (I can't seem to find one thin enough), I follow Neil in heading to them directly. When we arrive at that far-off place, the fifteen- or twenty-foot unpruned masses form the center of the largest backcountry cemetery we have ever found.

⟋ Despite a 1928 statement from Virginia officials that "residents will not be molested"; despite a letter in 1934 from Carson expressing that the removal of park residents was one of the most difficult and one of the "most humane undertakings"; despite a press release from the commission concluding that "ruthless methods should be avoided" and that "every consideration of humanity was being observed in obtaining possession of the park lands" and that "no inhabitant need suffer any undue hardships"; and despite an admonishment from the Archdeaconry of the Blue Ridge that "this wholesale depopulation of the park area seems . . . to be inconsistent with the humane policy adopted by the present Administration," what played out was not so humane for the more than twenty families who were physically removed from where they lived, with their homes burned to the ground.

Kenneth Shifflet and his family were some of the people evicted against their will, as residents and farmers of one parcel and owners and farmers of another. I first met Kenneth Shifflet, with his wife Anne, at the Shenandoah National Park ranger station at Simmons Gap, a parting of the hills near Flattop Mountain, which many Shiflets remember as the name of their ancestors' home place.

Back in the day, the Simmons Gap Episcopal Mission was a central meeting place for all the communities nearby, with a telephone for emergencies, a post office, and a "clothing bureau," or secondhand shop, where parents often outfitted children's wardrobes. Today, the mission's old recreation center—a long, rectangular stone building with a side porch and a patched-up outline of where the arched front doorway used to be—is a ranger's office, surrounded by a variety of sheds and outbuildings where kids once played marbles after church. The flat area that was once a baseball diamond where little Kenneth Shifflet and his friends and brothers played "town ball" every Sunday after church is a patch of thick woods that includes several chestnut stumps leftover from the chestnut blight, when foresters' best (but bad) advice to stem the disease was to cut every last chestnut down. When Kenneth Shifflet—now an unbelievably young-looking eighty-year-old with still mostly brown hair and smooth skin—looks at the fortress of trees surrounding this spot, he still sees the rolling fields, cleared far and wide, with his childhood home in the distance just on the other side of the gap.

"December 5, 1935," he blurted out when we met, as if he'd recited this date many times before, the calendar of events that transpired in his young life burned into his mind like a brand. "That's the day we left our home."

He had spent his first five years of life in the mountains; his father owned 325 acres and had lived on the mountain since his birth in about 1874. Kenneth described the land he grew up on as orchards of apples, cherries, peaches, and pears; bluegrass pasture; a kitchen garden with potatoes, cabbage, and turnips; and 150 head of sheep, which they sheared for wool. His father Ambrose sold trees for timber and peeled bark for a nearby tannery. He also grew wheat, oats, and corn, milled nearby and used for cooking. He raised cattle, hogs, and chickens for meat, milk, and eggs; and the family sold potatoes, sweet potatoes, onions, cabbages, and chestnuts door-to-door in the nearby city of Harrisonburg from Ambrose's wagon.

At home, his mother made hay beans by picking green beans and drying them in the sun. He also remembers schnitz—dried apples made the same way, which was a popular custom throughout the mountains. Mothers and kids everywhere on the mountain remember peeling and slicing Albemarle pippins, yorks, winesaps, or milams, laying them on the roof and making sure to collect them before the next rain.

The government started coming around Ambrose's place in the late 1920s, Kenneth said, during the period in which the government was surveying the land considered for the park, to determine boundary lines, the value of the land, the species of orchards and commercial timber. On each inventory report, inspectors made a note of Ambrose's wishes: "I do not care to sell." Nevertheless, Ambrose's tracts remained within the planned park boundary, and the government was clear with Ambrose in many notices and warnings that he had to leave. For months, years, Ambrose ignored attempts to get him to abandon his mountain home and the land he purchased piece by piece through toil and sweat.

On December 2, 1935, Ambrose dictated to his daughter a last-ditch letter to President Roosevelt, asking for help in his great trouble. "I am sixty-four years old and my eyes is bad. . . . I more than appreciate it if you could save my house if there is anything you can do. Do it at once for I am here and no place to go. . . . We are pleading for help to save our land."

He did not wait for a reply. On December 5 he and the family moved the farm animals and most of the furniture down to the lowlands. Kenneth, two sisters still living at home, and their mom caught a ride in a wagon down the mountain to their new house, owned by Ambrose's oldest son, a place that Kenneth said, "Mom hated . . . and I did too." They had planned to come back the next day to collect the rest of their things.

When they arrived on December 6, everything was gone: their things, the walls, the floors, the house. Their home—the place where Ambrose had grown from young man to husband to father to old man, where he had made a home with his wife, where his children were born and raised—had been burned down to the ground, with every possession that was still on site, bee hives and all.

It wasn't the only one. Just two months earlier, on October 3, 1935, Melanchton Cliser—a slight, long-faced man with a big nose, age sixty-two—walked out to the filling station he owned with his wife to help some customers pulling up for gas. He didn't know they were plainclothes sheriffs and deputies, because surely if he did, he would have stayed inside or shot them.

The men who came to the Cliser compound reportedly showed up only upon the threat of contempt of court. It seemed they would have much rather paid their ten cents for a hefty piece of Mrs. Cliser's huckleberry pie. Instead, instructed by a judge, they caught Cliser by surprise—after months and years of Cliser resisting officials' attempts at appraising his property, refusing to allow the government to resettle him elsewhere, ignoring offers for a Special Use Permit to allow him to remain on his land awhile—and handcuffed him for refusing to leave his home. Before four deputies wrestled him into the sheriff's car, Cliser "stood proudly in handcuffs and delivered a 'quavering' rendition of the entire Star-Spangled Banner," then delivered a speech about defending his rights, rights guaranteed by the Magna Carta and the U.S. Constitution. His wife remained on the gingerbread front porch of their high-class home, and the men removed the family's belongings from the house to the road and boarded it up.

"My father believed in the Constitution," Cliser's daughter said years later. "He'd never thought something like that could happen in America."

Eviction proceedings were issued for at least twenty families, a decision of the commonwealth as a method to handle those who would not leave any other way.

Twenty days after Ambrose found the remains of his home in ash and forty-one years after businesses and conservationists and governments began dreaming of and planning a park in the southern Appalachians to protect the eastern forests, after nine presidential administrations and twenty-one congresses, the nation did finally receive its twenty-third national park. (Great Smoky Mountains National Park was established in 1934 but was not officially dedicated until September 2, 1940.) Referred to by some as "the impossible park," Shenandoah became the largest national park in the East, with 181,547 acres encompassing nearly 2,000 parcels of land. Ambrose Shifflett's land—the center of his family's world—became a buffer around a two-mile section of Skyline Drive, dissected by an indistinct gravel fire road, just as Melanchton Cliser's land became a nameless, trailless area near the intersection of Skyline Drive and Route 211, where purportedly all that remains of his territory are the daylilies his wife had planted.

Kenneth—a man who can still do a full-body demonstration of how to sheer a sheep—went on to finish high school, obtain a college degree, and complete additional graduate school education. He became an associate professor at a university. He believes leaving was good for him because it allowed him to have more opportunities. Otherwise, he says, "I would have just been a 'mountain boy.'"

His family has never come back to partake of the park.

This backwoods cemetery, like all historic cemeteries, is a museum. The odd-shaped fieldstones, leaning headstones, primitive rock slabs with names and dates scratched in by hand—a custom for at least a 150 years in this area—are the framed artworks of the lives and backstories we will never really know. The triangles, rounded tops, square tops, and pointy tops; the tall ones and short ones; and the nearby indentations in the earth—decay—make the viewer ponder the canvas, estimate the landscape, imagine a life once lived here, a home once built, a spring, a barn, schools, neighbors, and a community, in the mind's eye.

We don't exactly know where to begin when we arrive. The cemetery is said to span fifty feet by fifty feet—it may have once been bordered by a fence—and it is said to be filled with more than fifty burials. There's Edward Shifflett, born 1864, died 1890, carved with imperfect handwriting, letters of different sizes. C. W. Powell, who died in 1878; Rebecca A. Shiflett, born 1845, died 1879; and M. M. Shiflett, who died in 1876, are all carved with great care with a steady hand, using horizontal lines like we were taught in grade school, for perfection, and the added flourish of diamond-shaped dots in between each word.

Some of the epitaphs, worn away with time and wind and acid rain, are illegible. Others were never carved in the first place or include only initials. Many are entombed inside the thick shelter of fat boxwoods, and Neil surprises me by getting down on all fours or on his back and crawling or slithering inside the stinky bushes to get a look at and read me the inscriptions hidden inside that he knows I want to hear.

As far from any other park visitors as we feel we are in this deep pocket of backcountry, we are surprised to find that not everything is old here. Someone has been here recently, perhaps coming in by one of the two old roads, marked on a 1929 map, that lead onto this property from privately owned land below. Behind the boxwoods are two new graves—as of 2007, according to Len Wheat: polished-granite, lapidary-inscribed, professionally made tombstones. Two feet tall, side by side, they are placed up against the original, more primitive stones that once marked these two men, with small, sun-faded, slightly ragged Confederate flags in the ground on stakes. They are Pvt. Elias Powell, CSA, 1838–October 30, 1862, "Killed by Union Cavalry Scouts," and Pvt. W. Albert Powell, CSA, May 27, 1841–May 10, 1864, "Killed in Action, Spotsylvania Courthouse," two of many Rebel dead we two native Yanks have found in these hills.

The day has become long at this point. We are far away from our car. It is three in the afternoon. We have made a first pass through the cemetery, but we haven't even started looking for the house site or the well Wheat describes. Back to my pack-too-much-into-one-day self, we had made tentative plans to hear a Shenandoah National Park scholar lecture this same afternoon, and I know we would need to leave soon to get there in time. Do I stay here, outdoors in the fresh air, or do I hike out to sit sedentary in a fluorescent-lighted room and imagine it instead?

I decide to stay in the park, not to rush and not to leave. By the end of the day, we will have returned on the old road we couldn't find in the beginning, and we will have explored the house site and the well and the white roofing material and the bathtub that had eluded us too. We will have sat down on the bare ground along the way at an overlook to rest, put our boots up on a rock, and talked about things a husband and wife who have been together for nearly twenty years only find time to talk about when they are away from the business of everyday life, when he is glad not to have to give his wife daily intravenous fluids and fix her meals and she is grateful not to require them, and I will feel healed by how the day has unfolded.

Being here, this real place in real life where people lived and died and where they were never allowed to return, at a destination hard to find and where we'll probably never come again, makes me feel alive with longing and love and life, makes me thirsty to move forward toward all that I have left to learn and live, here in this park and everywhere else. I have trusted Neil in leading us here, and in the process, I have come closer to trusting myself again. I am alive and hiking and relishing my body again—synapses, sensation, muscles, and movement. This body that I didn't know, this body that had abandoned me, this body (like land, I suppose—the only precious thing I'll ever own) had come back.

A Room at Killahevlin

Dear Mr. Secretary: We are nearing the point when we will
be ready to write a deed for the Shenandoah National Park
to the National Park Department, but the same old question arises—what are we going to do about the people living
within the area?

—WILLIAM E. CARSON to Secretary of the Interior Harold L.
Ickes, April 1934

I HAVE FINALLY MADE THE TRIP to Killahevlin, a
seventeen-room, four-chimney, seven-fireplace Edward-
ian limestone mansion with arts and crafts touches, on
three manicured, grassy acres, built on the highest hill in
Front Royal, Virginia, in 1905, overlooking the working-
class homes that fill this small Blue Ridge Mountain
town. It is the home that William E. Carson built: "a man
of vision" and of "amazing drive and resourcefulness," "a
pioneer," someone who displayed "dazzling imaginative
power," who gave years of "unselfish service," according
to the obituaries that ran in the local papers in 1942, six
years after the opening of Shenandoah National Park.

Here at Killahevlin—named after a favorite childhood
place in Carson's native Ireland, from which he had
emigrated at age fifteen—my purpose is to understand
the man behind the curtain, to inhabit his space, to
explore my curiosity about him. I am as caught up as I
ever have been, since learning the broad brushstroke of
the park story, in what I see as the evil of his deeds: set-

ting in motion the eminent domain condemnation of private mountain land to avoid personal negotiations with individuals; calling the forced purchase of ancestral land—motherland, home-is-where-the-heart-is land—from thousands of people a "cold business matter"; not involving the residents as stakeholders in the negotiations and plans for the changes that would dispossess them. More than anything, though, I am flummoxed as to the kind of man who would allow for the manhandling, handcuffing evictions, and house burnings that ultimately took place to get the people out of the park area and how such a responsible, honorable, methodical man—the man in charge—could have ended up so unprepared for dealing with the only true humanitarian issue involved with creating the park: how to handle the people who lived there.

The current owners of Carson's house (now a bed and breakfast), Tom and Kathy Conkey, have been gracious enough to give me a tour, tell me of some of the home's secrets and history, and open some of its vaults. They explain that the second-floor sunporch, now ablaze with more than a dozen bright windows, was an open veranda until the 1920s; that Carson's grounds were once three times larger; that they as innkeepers live in what was once the servants' quarters; and that before Carson even arrived at this high spot, years before he had come to America, Union soldiers encamped here. One night in the 1860s—as they were wont to do with men they saw as guerilla fighters—those Union soldiers hung two of Mosby's Rangers from a black walnut tree here. The tree is gone, but its last remaining seedling still grows in the front yard.

The center of the house is grand—an angled-wall fireplace in the receiving room, a living room and dining room with wide pocket doors, a sunporch morphed into an Irish pub. Carson planned to build an elevator in the three-story home but never finished, but the two-story guest house out back that housed presidents and movie actors indicates the Carsons' financial and social standing in the community. Carson's immigrant father built this town, after all, mining lime.

Tom ushers me to sit at one of the many small tables set up for guests in the dining room, with a view of Shenandoah National Park out the four large windows, and he brings out a crumbling old photo album and scrapbook—Carson's personal story, found in an attic in Oregon by one of Carson's daughter's nephews. Inside are pictures of black nannies dressed in white petticoats taking care of Carson's children on the front porch, a note from a French maid asking for more money, blueprints from when Carson designed the house with the Washington DC architects who also designed the Old Executive Office Building, and photos of Carson over time, from a young man with thick wavy brown hair and pudgy cheeks to an older man with lighter hair, round glasses, and jowls.

Tom says that the former town manager of Front Royal knew Carson. "He told me he was the nicest guy," Tom recalls. "Outgoing and a good businessman." I heard the same thing when I talked with the wife of one of Carson's great-nephews in Virginia. "It was a close-knit family," she told me, "and we heard about Will all the time."

"Carson didn't want to push the people out," she said of the residents that had to be removed to create the park, "but maybe I'm seeing it the way I wanted to see it."

When I spoke with Walter Duncan myself, the former town manager who served for twenty-two years and has now passed away, he said Carson was "old" in the 1930s and 1940s, when the manager was a kid. "I knew him around the lime plant. A nice man, a very fine gentleman. Everyone liked him in the county, but not everyone in the park liked him."

But "it needed to be done," he said of buying people's land for the park.

John F. Horan Jr., former editor of the *Northern Virginia Daily*, who did his master's thesis on William E. Carson in 1977, chimed in as well. "I never came across anything suggesting Carson had qualms about the dislocations the park project would cause," he said. "I think Carson and Co. viewed that as a fair process."

Tom also tells me that Carson's granddaughter-in-law was a recent guest at the bed and breakfast. He told her about my research and the fact that I maintained "popular misconceptions" about Carson, as being "single-minded and brusque."

"She confirmed he was a real family man," he says as evidence of Carson's character.

My mission, I tell Tom, is to uncloak Carson, to look beyond the platitudes, beyond the pain I feel his worthy project caused for the people of the mountains, and to understand him as a man. Tom lays it out simple: Carson was just doing his job, and "when you make an omelet, you break a few eggs."

I admit, Carson knew how to get a job done—he had tenacity. And it *was* a job, after all. Despite the fact that purchasing the people's land wound up costing more than he expected, and fundraising dollars were fewer than he expected, and boundary lines among property tracts and proof of ownership were less clear than expected, he continued with the job. When state funding threatened to dry up, and the acreage of the park was cut to less than half of the vision of the original dreamers, and the whole project looked like it would blow up, he continued with the job.

"Quitting never accomplishes anything," he once said.

In fact, Carson found some creative ways to secure the project, to get the nation attached to the coming park and to see it as inevitable. Knowing President Herbert Hoover was a trout man—"[Fishing] is a constant reminder of the democracy of life . . . for all men are created equal before fishes," the president said—Carson secured the fishing rights on ten thousand acres, thanks to a surveyor working for him who "used all the arguments, influence, and resources that I could command," and lured the president to establish a "summer White House," or fishing camp, in the Blue Ridge Mountains within the proposed park boundaries.

Better yet, by getting Hoover into the park, Carson got the first stages of Skyline Drive underway, which became a no-turning-back milestone for the whole grand plan and the number-one way that most visitors experience the park even today. Back in 1924 the committee responsible for choosing a park site had said that "the greatest single feature . . . is a possible sky-line drive along the mountaintop." One evening, while riding horseback with the second National Park Service director Horace M. Albright, Hoover is rumored to have said, "I think everybody ought to have a chance to get the views from here. I think they're the greatest in the world." He then directed Albright to "talk it over with Carson."

Carson then set up the first two national-park Civilian Conservation Corps camps in Shenandoah and got the project started.

Carson believed in the cause—preserving the forests and fauna of the Blue Ridge for Americans in perpetuity, preventing future development and destruction—and who can blame him? Carson eloquently described the park as a place with "matchless scenic wonders," with scenery that "mak[es] pictures . . . no camera or painter could reproduce," and his work to preserve it came with immediate rewards. "Your commission has helped to save our wild life from hunters," an assistant federal naturalist told him once the park was secured. "Only by your prompt action and ready cooperation was preservation possible."

Nevertheless, during the eight years of his service in creating the park, Carson considered the project a nightmare because of all the problems that surfaced along the way. "This awful Shenandoah National Park undertaking," he called it, lamenting that it was "a disagreeable and abhorrent job." During those "eight weary years" of work, his hair turned from black to white.

"Only the strictest sense of duty and patriotic desire for the good of the people of the state" kept the commission going, he said. "If the Park will give the people of Virginia half the enjoyment it gave us anxiety and tribulation it will be a mountain of content."

Could Carson have ever imagined that, instead of the mountains and views and waterfalls and streams, the lure that would draw some hikers to the park seventy-five years later would be the history of the dispossessed? I can't imagine that he did, that he could see the hunt for the lost communities as a pastime of significant merit and longevity to make a lifetime's passion. And yet finding the old country lanes, the barbed wire fence on the edges of old fields, the big old trees lining a boundary, the apple trees still fruiting in old orchards is the reason I and the other few bushwhackers of the park come back again and again. The shadow of the former life is still sketched upon the landscape, and I can still uncover it, be surprised by it, and be taught by it. That I still ask questions about it—still question my own part in acquiescing to the arrangement, still wonder if, hiking here, I am a silent party to the gambit—has been the source of twenty years of joy and wonder.

In my mellower moments, I feel a soft spot for Carson. People like George Freeman Pollock misled him—and many others—into thinking the land wasn't populated. The early business promoters didn't have an accurate handle on the value of the land or the people's tenacious attachment to it. Things kept changing on Carson, and he kept having to adapt. Although Ray Lyman Wilbur, secretary of the interior under President Hoover from 1929 to 1933, made a promise to park residents—sending them all letters to this effect—that they would not be asked to move unless they were in in the direct path of development, such as Skyline Drive, the new National Park Service director, Cammerer, rescinded that promise in the 1930s. He decided that all inhabitants would have to vacate before turning the area into a park. "We must aim at a real park and not a make-believe one cluttered up with tenants and land occupants," he said, the poorest of whom, incidentally, he called "scum"—seemingly one of the biggest switcheroos pulled on Carson, who had to deal with the fallout.

"It is not very good faith to change policy," Carson wrote.

On the other hand, it seems Carson may have known what would ultimately be done. As early as 1928, as assistant director of the National Park Service, Cammerer had expressed his view that no private residences should remain. In 1929 Carson wrote, "We have quite a responsibility in taking over the Park toward the people whose homes are there, as we turn them loose in the world." And he wondered who would take care of the cemeteries after residents left. But records show that when Carson heard about Cammerer's new rule, he called it a "very difficult problem that suddenly arose."

Carson came up with a solution for Cammerer's final decision: while Cammerer and administrators tried to figure out just what exactly to do with all the people who had not left the soon-to-be park lands as of 1933—those who were not yet part of the diaspora of mountain communities and culture—Carson ran an internment camp of sorts.

"Resistance was encountered at every point," Carson said of his park experience. "It was not to our taste or liking to dispossess thousands of people from their lands . . . or to be at dagger's point with our mountain neighbors. . . . Time and time again we were threatened with sudden death by infuriated landowners."

Those who didn't think the commonwealth was offering enough money for their land ("ruinous values," according to one landowner) but were planning to move after seeing an arbitrator to plead their case were not really Carson's problem: "Neither I nor the State Conservation and Development Commission . . . have anything whatsoever to do with the assessment and determination of the value of these lands. That is wholly in the hands of the Courts and Appraisal Commissioners appointed by the Courts. All we can do is to accept or reject the awards made by the Courts," Carson told one of the 133 landowners who was not satisfied with the prices set on his land and who went to arbitration.

Many of the people who remained were those who were not interested in selling at any price and had no intention of leaving, and they *were* Carson's problem.

"Incredible as it may appear," wrote the *New York Times* in January 1934 in an article called "$900,000 Goes Begging for Somebody to Take It," about this very group, "there are scores, if not hundreds, of property owners . . . who seemingly do not want money which belongs to them."

Carson's problem also included those who were simply too poor to move—the tenants or squatters on land they didn't own—and those who had nowhere else to go. Of the 465 families remaining in 1934 (2,300 people), 197 of them owned their own land, and 268 of them, or 58 percent, owned no equity in their house or land and would not benefit from any payouts from the government or resettlement housing.

Miriam Sizer, of Corbin Hollow infamy, believed that as nonvoting citizens (in the 1930s in Virginia, as in much of the South, illiterate people—blacks and whites—with taxable property less than $250 were not eligible to vote), the mountain residents had been powerless to advocate for themselves over the years to gain access to state-funded public schools or to benefit from improved roads. She suggested that the federal government resettle these folks in homesteads in nearby lowlands. "May it not be that this Shenandoah National Park movement, coordinating both State and Federal forces may be the means of great Civic Justice in our country?" she asked.

Carson pooh-poohed the idea: "To go through what this woman proposes would mean years of work and trouble," he had said.

But it was Carson's job to figure it out. He knew he needed a sound plan, a decent plan, to get the people out and that the only alternative to such a plan was large-scale eviction. "And neither you nor I," he beseeched the Virginia governor and members of the State Commission on Conservation and Development, whom he hoped would come up with a plan, "on whom the responsibility would eventually fall, would care to be party to the eviction of three hundred and forty families—more than eighteen hundred (1,800) people—in the depths of a depression. If we did, we no doubt would be charged with inhumanity."

How do I feel being in Carson's house? I feel the impact of the disparity in wealth between how he lived and the lifestyle of many of the mountain residents whom he displaced. Killahevlin is large and luxurious—opulent, even, with its ornate baseboard, window, and crown moldings; its two staircases; numerous bedrooms and bathrooms; the stone walls around the perimeter—especially compared to the rustic, one-room log homes like Jones Mountain Cabin, Corbin Cabin, and those I've seen so many times in historical photos of the park, government photos that were skewed toward portraying the poor. Killahevlin is an estate, a landmark—on the National Registry of Historic Places and the Virginia Landmarks Register. The homes in the park—made with rough, ready materials—were considered to be worth nothing at the time of park creation and were mostly burned or torn down or "left to mold away," so as not to mar visitor views.

By early 1934 Carson had been required to attend and coordinate ten to fifteen meetings to discuss purchasing land for resettlement homesteads and building the new homes—what wound up taking the form of small, boxy white houses that still stand in some form today. (One former resettlement resident described them as "very lightly put up. Wind'd blow, they just rattle and shake, you could just naturally feel 'm rock." "No interaction with nature, and no front porch," another descendant told me, indicating values of importance.) The government would wind up purchasing 6,200 acres of land—enough, they believed, to accommodate both part- and full-time farmers—as seven planned communities in nearby valley towns, each with a designated Resettlement Road or Homestead Road, still named as such on street signs today. Some houses came with running water and electricity, and some did not. Qualified people could rent them for $5 a year ($87 in 2013) and eventually buy them with low-income, long-term mortgages. But the mortgage details were never really explained to some residents and thus caused foreclosures and evictions many years down the line. Some families had a mortgage for the first time but no jobs or cars, as they had been used to living off the land. Other families hated living there so much, they tried to move back to their mountain homes.

Those who were too poor for rent and mortgages were handled as welfare cases, and those who were too proud to accept help—descendant Elisabeth Weakley said her family "would have been scandalized to have even considered a relocation camp; mountaineers don't want to be beholden to anyone"—were left to fend for themselves. Some eagerly awaited their new resettlement homes—"Do you think I am going to hate having running water in my home, and a smooth yard with green grass, a store close by and the electric?" one woman asked. Others dreaded the move to a new place, a place one descendant described as "more alien than Mars."

Anyone who remained on the land as of 1933, waiting for the new government homesteads or otherwise, had to obtain a Special Use Permit, issued by the State Commission on Conservation and Development and approved by Carson, a compromise he brokered to address Secretary Wilbur's letter to residents. Carson argued that the letter had been written, after all, "for the purpose of inducing the people to go along with the Park movement."

These permits, which allowed them to remain on their land, use their own buildings, reap what crops they had already cultivated that year, but cultivate no additional land, expired November 1, 1934. They were reissued in 1935, then 1936, then 1937—even after the national park opened to the public. Then in 1938 and again in 1939, because of the state and federal government's bureaucracy and ineptitude in getting its resettlement and emergency programs organized. Each year, the government thought it had the resettlement problem licked, but the reality was that the land purchases for the resettlement communities, the resettlement housing, and plans for welfare care kept being transferred from one agency to the next—from the Civil Works Administration under the Federal Emergency Relief Administration to the Subsistence Homesteads Division of the U.S. Department of the Interior, to the federal Resettlement Administration, to the federal Farm Security Administration in the U.S. Department of Agriculture, and then to Virginia's Emergency Relief Administration—after each one failed to fulfill its commitments to the project and the people.

"Near-chaos," is how one early park employee described the situation.

"United only in their failure to acknowledge the impact of their policy on human life and their serene conviction of that policy's righteousness" is one researcher's indictment of the agencies involved.

Residents were allowed to continue using milk cows in certain designated areas of the park, in the same area they had grazed before but nowhere else and for no other reason other than their own personal use. No living timber could be harvested or destroyed. They could not cut new sod. They could not hunt or fish. Only livestock that were fenced in could graze, and no begging from park visitors or solicitation was allowed. The manufacture or sale of liquor was prohibited and would void the permit instantly. Essentially, any of the residents' most recent industry that provided an income was prohibited—no matter that the doomed chestnut trees, the massive drought, and other changes to the forest resources had already whittled down workers' options. Not to mention the fact that the park closed nearly all cross-mountain roads leading from one side of the range to the other, forcing everyone in the vicinity to make long detours around these new public grounds.

Because all the homes, barns, sheds, outbuildings, farms, orchards, and gardens were now government land, the people had to ask permission to prune their own apple trees, harvest their own apples, remove building materials such as roofing and lumber and barbed wire from abandoned homes to use for their own needs, or cultivate a private garden, corn, or other crops. One man asked whether he could move into Robert H. Via's old house, which sat vacant. Two different men asked whether they could plant their gardens on Ambrose Shifflet's unused land. Sometimes the government said yes; sometimes it said no.

As the land transitioned from state control to federal administration, different officials responded to different letters, giving widely varied answers. Neither William E. Carson nor Wilbur C. Hall, Carson's successor, who were hired to handle land acquisition and management, nor J. R. Lassiter—hired in 1933 as the engineer in charge to supervise construction of the Appalachian Trail through Shenandoah and to manage the construction of Skyline Drive, a man who was primarily an engineer and highway man but who became park superintendent in 1937—nor R. Taylor Hoskins, chief ranger at the park's inception and later superintendent as well, nor even Cammerer, the third National Park Service director, had come up with a plan of action for handling the remaining residents and their daily needs. Nor were any of them trained in managing people per se. None of the men involved from the beginning had investigated how many people lived on the land and what exactly to do with them once the park came to life. The park itself had been their only concern.

So the men played favorites with the residents, taking away rights from people they thought had misbehaved and granting privileges to those they felt were worthy. Lassiter answered the letter of one resident, who asked to farm a garden, with, "You have not co-operated in any way and have refused to sign permits at all times, therefore, nothing at all can be done for you at any time." To another, he wrote, "If you do not change your attitude and give [a welfare worker] the proper co-operation, we will be forced to secure a writ of eviction and put you out of the park."

When a resettlement official requested that the remaining mountain families be allowed to use firewood from the park, as they had no other way to obtain fuel, Lassiter responded, "We have already done much more work on the movement of these families than was originally contemplated. . . . I do not feel that it is our responsibility to furnish them with wood, and I think that the sooner they realize that they have to support themselves, the better for all concerned."

In response to another park resident, however, a business owner who asked to be able to store equipment on park land until his new establishment was ready (after being denied the ability to keep his business going in the park), Cammerer wrote, "I regard [the man] as a square-shooter and a good neighbor, and as he is willing to do the right thing I am glad to meet him more than halfway."

Sometimes the answers seemed arbitrary. On March 26, 1936, J. R. Lassiter answered a letter from one man, telling him he could go ahead and raise his garden that year. Seven days later, on April 3, 1936, J. R. Lassiter answered a letter from someone else, telling her that he could not give her permission to cultivate any of her land within the park, because "I have to observe the rules and regulations."

⌒ In the end, Carson's staff did not devise a successful plan for resident removal, despite all that he had successfully achieved to put the park into motion.

At this critical moment, some people inside and outside the State Commission on Conservation and Development began demanding a reorganization of the commission. The commission had come under fire by former Virginia governor and later U.S. senator Harry F. Byrd, the man who had hired Carson for the job in the first place. Byrd and Carson did not agree on when the park should open—given that Skyline Drive was not complete—and whether Carson's brother should be paid for the legal assistance he provided during the Shenandoah development process. Byrd involved himself in details Carson wished he wouldn't, about when and how the landowners should be paid, urging the project along to bring in revenue for the state, rather than abiding by the orderly and carefully timed progression of things as Carson had wished. They were details that would fray the relationship between them.

Carson ultimately proposed the commission's reorganization. His proposal changed his own chairmanship position from a part-time advisory role—which he had served in a way that was "entirely nonpolitical [with] every thought being for the good of the State, regardless of political effects"—to a full-time salaried position designated by the governor. Newspapers and others speculated about whether the new governor, Governor Peery, would reappoint Carson for this redefined position, calling him "obviously and conspicuously the ideal man for the post."

But the disagreements with Senator Byrd cast a pall over the appointment. To calm the political furor over whether or not he'd be appointed, Carson, who had already been put through the ringer with the Shenandoah park project and who did not have political ambitions, excused himself from being considered for the chairmanship again.

He said he wanted to spend more time being president and general manager of the lime business his father had started. He wrote to a colleague that the reorganization of the commission would "honorably relieve me of work that . . . has in it more disagreeable elements than anything that has ever been undertaken in the State." He also said that he found the political nature of the new position "nauseating," and so he resigned at the end of 1934, in the thick of the resident-removal disaster, his hands mostly clean.

The winds of change swept in after Carson's departure. It was Wilbur C. Hall, a lawyer and state legislator, who became the new chairman of the State Commission on Conservation and Development, and it was he who decided on eviction as "a last resort." He was the catalyst for Ambrose Shifflett's house being burned down one day before he fully vacated it and for the call to handcuff and remove Melanchton Cliser, owner of the gas station and store within the park boundary who did not want to leave.

Hall and new National Park Service employee J. R. Lassiter had ordered twenty such uncooperative families evicted, as they "refused all efforts to get them to sign permits."

The evictions continued through at least 1937, despite letters from the public to President and Mrs. Roosevelt and federal officials that had been prompted by a slew of articles in local and national papers describing the events. The letters admonished that "ground for a national park cannot be so urgently needed that three sick people have to be taken out of their beds and carried to the poorhouse . . . in the rain," as one newspaper reported—actions that "can hardly be justified by law when they fell so short of humanity."

The evictions continued despite park visitors pleading that the residents "feel very bad to leave their mountain homes which I feel is as dear to them as yours and mine" and despite pleas that "acts of unkindness do not solve their problem."

While one newspaper reported that Hall believed the process of moving hundreds of residents from their homes "was painful to both the residents and to those charged with moving them," records show a hand-scribbled message in a government file, on a clipping of one of these sad human-interest stories, saying, "Who wrote this sob-story stuff?"

When people pointed fingers to the state for carrying out such ghastly evictions, the state pointed to Washington DC as the driving force behind it, since the federal government refused to accept inhabited land. The feds pushed back on this assertion, falling back on its original stance that it was merely in the position of receiving state lands as a donation, or gift. A memorandum from Herbert Brooks, chief of the National Park Service Land Division, even documents that "the fundamental and basic facts in this proposition are, first, the Federal Government will not accept title to the land within the proposed Shenandoah National Park area until these residents are completely removed from the area. Second, the National Park Service will insist that this is the duty of the State of Virginia and that the Park Service will not have any responsibility in the matter."

A Western Union telegram received December 5, 1935, from Hall to Cammerer confirms the state's deference to the feds. Hall says, the "Sheriff . . . has just called this office . . . advising that the few families against whom he has eviction orders have no place to go. We have advised him that we are unable to grant any concessions. Of course, if you desire to communicate with [the] Sheriff . . . and permit him to allow these people to remain, there is no objection on our part. We are just attempting to carry out your requirements for taking over the park."

The feds didn't stop any of the evictions, and the never-never land in which both entities existed meant that neither party had to accept responsibility for its actions.

As for Carson, there is no one left to say what exactly he thought or did during this terrible time, as his daughters destroyed most his personal papers, thinking the material was duplicated elsewhere. No one knows what was in his heart. Only one point is clear: after 1934 Carson could thank God that Shenandoah was not his problem anymore.

There is one particular room at Killahevlin that Tom Conkey wants to show me. It is a room I will spend the weekend in, breathing in Carson's air, looking out at Carson's views. I am not aware of any special significance of the room, so I follow his lead.

It is on the second floor at the top of the stairs, a twenty-five–by–fifteen–foot space with a stained glass transom; ornate lovebird-and-floral-motif wallpaper in white, green, and raspberry; a pink settee; and four large windows.

This was Carson's study, Tom says; though, there are no traces of Carson in this room I can discern, nothing masculine at all.

Near the fireplace, at the edge of the tile surround, he indicates a mark on the otherwise unmarred oak hardwood floors. "Do you know what this is from?" he asks. I shake my head.

"When the previous owners bought the house, this fireplace was boarded up, and this corner was framed out as a closet," he explains. I imagine this corner of the room with a door on a hinge and a knob, with the hidden fireplace in the back of the dark space perhaps used for off-season clothes or storage. "They tore out the closet walls to reveal the fireplace again and found that a supporting beam had damaged the floorboards."

"They say," he continues, "that Carson's son used to sit near this fireplace and do his homework while Carson looked on and worked at his desk." I imagine Carson coming home from a day at work, settling here in his home office—known as the library or coffee room in its time—working on leftover issues from the day, poring over new maps of uncharted country, and conducting back-of-the-envelope calculations of prices and payments, sweating the inconsistencies in numbers, with his sweet young son within view.

The story hangs in the air like a deflated balloon. I had not heard any stories about Carson's son. I did not know the significance of the moment. In fact, I had not really thought about Carson as a family man at all until this visit, about his having a private life outside of his work. It was not until Tom showed me a manila folder with the obituaries that I understood.

"After young Billy's death," Tom continues, "it is said that Carson couldn't bear the sight of the fireplace again, so he boarded it up."

The newspaper clippings, soft and yellowed, dated 1925, say it all. I find in print that in the year before Governor Byrd selected him for the chairmanship of the State Commission for Conservation and Development, before Carson had ever dreamed of his intense involvement in creating Shenandoah National Park, three years before the invention of antibiotics, just a few weeks after celebrating Christmas and New Years in Richmond with family, and a few months before a planned high school graduation celebration, Carson's only son, age sixteen, came down with influenza and double pneumonia and died.

"Death Strikes Hard Blow," one obituary headline reads from the *Daily Independent.* "W. E. Carson, Jr., 16, Dies at Home from Pneumonia," says the other. "Young 'Billy' Carson . . . who embodied with rare fidelity the Spirit of Youth standing upon the threshold of life, with the world to win—his soul astir with high aspirations and dreams of great achievement—was stricken by the cold hand of death. . . . His death has literally broken up a home."

In the silent, numb moments it takes me to absorb these words, I transform from seeing Carson as a man of privilege and a man who is all about business to seeing him as real flesh and blood, a man who lived his everyday life in this house, as a husband, as a father, and as a mourner. A suffering man. A man who knew a terrible loss.

The story of the study is a secondhand, thirdhand, or fourthhand account, a legend, a myth, a tiny piece in the entirety of the terrible tale. But in hearing it, I find myself swayed in a direction I could not have imagined at the start of my journey. I see for the first time that Carson, the father, the husband, the man, the fallible human, must have known what it was like to lose part of your soul, to feel powerless against forces you cannot control, to have to learn how to live again when you feel everything has been taken, to have to keep living with the burden of an unimaginable and incurable loss.

Knowing this piece of personal information alone could have been enough to soften my view of Carson's heart, but a few weeks later I visit an archive to comb through Carson's correspondence as chairman of the State Commission on Conservation and Development. It is there that I find an unusual letter typed and signed by his hand.

In all the business dealings Carson had with others— members of his commission; Harry F. Byrd, both as a governor and then as a senator; National Park Service directors, Albright and Cammerer among them—Carson was warm and engaging, even when businesslike and direct. In previous letters to Cammerer, in particular, Carson's salutation inevitably always read, "My dear Cam," and Cammerer returned the familiarity by calling him "Will." Carson frankly and honestly put forth his opinions of how plans for the park should and should not proceed. Though Cammerer was in a superior role to Carson overall, Carson did not subjugate himself to him.

In this one letter, though—perhaps the last letter Carson sent Cammerer, perhaps the last letter Carson sent anyone before leaving his post, perhaps his one final gesture to the world as a public figure—Carson used a different tone altogether. Maybe he thought others would read it in the future, but I rather think it was to underscore the gravity of his message.

In December 1934, just before his departure, Carson submitted to Cammerer a list of the people he suggested for lifetime residency in the park. The letter begins extremely formally, "Dear Sir," and continues:

> Enclosed herewith you will find a list of the people within the Park Area who, I recommend, should not, for humanitarian reasons, be moved.
>
> You will note their ages run from 60 to 90 years. Neither you nor I if we had lived in one place would like to be dispossessed at that age, and I know with

your kindly feeling toward old people, you will accede to this request on my part, that these dwellers within the Park Area will be undisturbed during their lifetime.

He goes on to mention a few of the people's names and where they live, showing their relative distance from Skyline Drive—to guarantee to Cammerer, no doubt, that they were far from where tourists could potentially see them.

It is in his closing that I really see Carson's soul.

No longer a man interested in the scientific and mathematical calculations of land assessments and payments, he appeals to Cammerer's emotional side, to the right brain, that which houses the arts and beauty and eschews reason and logic, to the cultivated man's familiarity with theater, with a line from Shakespeare's *The Merchant of Venice*. In an imperfect rendition likely called up from his memory, he writes:

The quality of mercy is not strained
It droppeth as a gentle due from Heaven
And is thrice blessed.

The notices to vacate had been sent to residents nearly a year earlier, and Carson could not know of the evictions that would come to pass a year after this letter. And so it was just this one thing, after all he had set in motion, such a small thing, that he asked for before he took his leave.

Perhaps he feared what would come next and what legacy he would leave. In this final moment, in what I perceive almost as a confession, as an act of repentance, maybe he wanted to know that he could live the rest of his life having done something right by the people he abandoned.

Indeed, there would come to pass a group of individuals who, unbeknownst to them during all the insanity, had won the golden ticket: they were selected to remain in the park to live out the rest of their lives. Despite the decision that "private occupancy of the lands is incompatible with their administration [as] a national park," Carson, Cammerer, Lassiter, and Secretary of the Interior Harold L. Ickes, together and separately, had decided that about forty elderly, infirm, and "meritorious" people could stay on the land forever. They had been placed on a secret list—the "Secretary's List," or the "Ickes List," named for the ultimate decision maker and savior.

Aside from age and disability, some on the list were chosen "as a matter of personal merit," giving weight to the belief that residents felt all along that how they were treated was related to how they were viewed by the people in power.

One man among the chosen was considered "above average."

Another, who had a wife and five children, was deemed "very good people."

Others were noted as "crippled but . . . decent and respectable," "excellent citizens," and "really desirable and deserving people."

Finnell Corbin, the patriarch of the last Corbin generation of Corbin Hollow, made it onto the lifetime list.

Lewis Willis, of the Landowners Protective Association, was also allowed to stay in his home—after the National Society of United States Daughters of 1812 lobbied on his behalf, claiming him as a lineal descendant of Betty Washington ("With so distinguished a family record, it would seem to me that it would but add dignity to this lovely section [of park] to have him remain"). He lived as a tenant on park land for more than twenty years, eventually engulfed by blindness and then death at age eighty-five, his once-cleared lawn already being taken over by saplings.

George Freeman Pollock, owner of Skyland, the man who lobbied for the park to be located at his doorstep as a way to boost his business, a man who may have never considered that the park he worked for and promoted would eventually buy up his property as well, depriving him of his mountain-resort livelihood, was allowed to live out the rest of his life as a tenant in one of his cottages until he died, after failing health, in 1949. An outside concessionaire took over the resort in 1937.

A woman named Annie Lee Bradley Shenk—a cousin of Melanchton Cliser, the man who was arrested at his store—and her much-older husband, who described themselves as "just as humble as we could be," were allowed to stay as well. Annie lived until age ninety-two, making her the longest-term resident of the park, until her death in 1978. To help her survive after her husband's passing in 1943, park staff stopped in to check on her and mow her lawn. Ultimately, rangers supplied her with wood, even trudging through waist-deep snow on foot one winter when they knew she'd run out of supplies. Records from 1950 show that the National Park Service distributed Christmas baskets donated by the Shenandoah Employees Association to her and all the others remaining in the park.

Others, however, were decidedly left off the list. For example, a handwritten note on an old letter in a government file says that another resident, Young Judd, who was part of a family that had purchased lots at Skyland resort, should be left out of the park area because he financed the Via U.S. Supreme Court case, which challenged the constitutionality of Carson's condemnation proceedings.

And so it went: the lucky and the losers.

On July 6, 1936, President Franklin Delano Roosevelt presided over a dedication ceremony attended by more than fifteen thousand visitors sitting on benches made from dead chestnuts cleared from the forests, with radio listeners across the nation. From a podium draped in red, white, and blue and decorated with a bald eagle, introduced with music from the U.S. Marine Band, Roosevelt offered the park to the American people as a "work of conservation" and a place for "recreation and re-creation."

"All across the Nation," he said, "at all times of the year, people are starting out for their vacations in national and state parks. Those people will put up roadside camps or pitch their tents under the stars, with an open fire to cook by, with the smell of the woods, and the wind in the trees. They will forget the rush and the strain of all the other long weeks of the year, and for a short time at least, the days will be good for their bodies and good for their souls."

Wilbur J. Hall, the man who came in at the tail end of a multidecade saga, received all the accolades for William E. Carson's work over the years. Meanwhile, Carson is said to have spent the rest of his life as "a political pariah," the state administration having severed all ties.

Within a year of Carson's resignation, Virginia's tourism trade had grown by $18 million, just as Carson had anticipated. The Commonwealth of Virginia would commemorate Carson's work by erecting a highway marker in his name in his adopted home town of Front Royal, Virginia, and the U.S. Board of Geographic Names—on behalf of Shenandoah National Park—would designate a nondescript 2,500-foot mountain in the park as Carson Mountain a few miles from his home. It is not a memorable mountain but one that I have hiked and on which I found an old, still-fruiting sour cherry tree from some long-ago home site, whose branches I reached and jumped toward, atop a high rock, in an effort to taste the gleaming red sweetness dangling appetizingly before me like candy.

But Carson needed no mountain. In a statement by Senator Harry F. Byrd Sr. about Carson upon his death in 1942, he said, "The establishment of Shenandoah National Park will always stand as a monument to him."

Carson is buried near the park among the entire Carson clan, in a simple family plot in Front Royal, where his wife, brothers, and children are all marked only by simple headstones with names and dates. There are no grand monuments, no inscriptions, no filigree. He could be anyone, or he could be no one. One warm winter day, I walk the grassy area enclosed by a concrete berm, and—after many years of doubt and distrust—I finally pay my respects. At the end of my journey of asking Carson, wherever he can still be found, to prove his intentions, taking him to my own private court to hear his posthumous defense, ultimately, in my mind, forever and in peace, I have set Carson free.

⌒ Timber Hollow Tale

SOME PEOPLE COME TO find the murder site. Others want to glimpse remnants of the old still, hidden in the woods where mountain men made moonshine. I have never attended an organized hike with the Potomac Appalachian Trail Club (PATC) before, but I've come to Shenandoah National Park, as I always do, for the dead.

Neil and I are new members of the club, having received its monthly newsletter with hike descriptions only once, and all I know about this excursion is that it is supposed to be an easy day of off-trail hiking through the once-inhabited Timber Hollow, a place I'd never heard of and had never been, on the west side of Skyline Drive, which we have much neglected for the east. We have been promised old wagon roads, a vintage baby carriage alongside the trail, and a cabin site.

The hike is to be led by Leonard Wheat, author of the bushwhacking guide that directed us to the lost cabins of Old Rag Mountain just weeks ago, hiker and bushwhacker extraordinaire, a man who probably knows the secrets of each ridge and each hollow better than anyone else alive. "First I hiked all the trails," he says, referring to the five hundred miles of maintained paths. "Then I got tired of taking the same trails over and over and decided to hike everything off trail," he says of the park's two hundred thousand acres.

Based on reading his bushwhacking book, I had envisioned Len as a grizzled mountain man—with a long unkempt beard and scraggly hair, dirty workpants, and the swollen fingers of someone who works outdoors. He is not anything like I expected: he's clean shaven; partly bald with white hair, and dressed in a wrinkle-free polyester collared shirt, a clean red jacket, slacks, and what seem like fine leather walking shoes. (He says he prefers Red Wings to big lug-sole boots.) He sports a bright-yellow baseball cap and has the thin, smooth hands of an office worker, which in fact he was—a Harvard PhD economist for the Department of Commerce in Washington DC. At age seventy-eight, his voice is extremely deep, he uses words like "swell," and he is the spitting image of Neil's late father, a no-nonsense guy with a hearty laugh. He sings jingles he remembers from the old days, with perfect pitch.

Baby faced, head wrapped in his white bandana, our now-dear friend Jeremy makes his first appearance in our lives at this hike. He explains he's also here because of Len, also planning to bushwhack the eighteen cabins of Old Rag next weekend with his brother Mike. He's been poking around in these and other woods since he was a kid, finding historic relics of human habitation as a pastime: he gets excited about old mines, fence posts, bits of barbed wire. I've met plenty of Civil War buffs who enjoy searching for belt buckles and buttons, and of course there are the arrowhead collectors and fossil hunters, but I had never met anyone else who named old fence posts as a fascinating item to find. In fact, I learn that Jeremy will flee to Shenandoah to go hunting in the woods for historical stuff any time he's not working his job managing fire- and water-damage restoration projects. I decide as soon as I hear these details that he will be my new best hiking buddy—after Neil, of course, who would pretty much rather be in the woods than anywhere else.

In meeting Len and Jeremy, as well as Bob Pickett—one of the PATC hike organizers, another lifetime hiker of the park, a naturalist with a knowledge of cultural history, and a frequent PATC hike leader—and Steve Bair, who at this time has been the park's backcountry, wilderness, and trails manager for twenty-five years and knows all about the park's hidden life, I cozy into a warm thought, something I have not been able to say thus far in all the years I've been exploring these woods: "I have found my people."

Gathered at the Timber Hollow Overlook in thirty-degree weather on a bright March Saturday, facing west into the Shenandoah Valley, our group of seventeen learns that Len has set one of our goals for the day as finding the site of the 1931 murder of Edward Buracker, a man who once lived on this ridge. With an icy sky hanging over the valley's undulating patchwork-farm landscape, Len reads a passage from a book written by George Freeman Pollock of Skyland resort. Buracker, a mountain resident and World War I veteran, he explains, was on his way home from retrieving his mail, when a group of men from Ida Hollow shot him through the heart for potentially exposing the location of an illegal still. According to the book, "The murderer then dragged the body a long distance to a ravine by the side of the trail and covered it with leaves and brush." With that introduction, Len tells us we're headed to the bloody site and we're going to find the location of the illegal still as well.

I had no expectations of the group that would attend this hike, and yet I am struck by the sea of gray hair. Len is the oldest. The average age of the group is probably fifty-five. Jeremy and I are among the youngest, in our thirties at the time. The older folks are carrying one or two ski-pole walking sticks each, and nearly everyone over fifty has tucked their pants into their socks, for fear of ticks, I presume.

The women are well attired in moisture-wicking fabrics, fleece, name-brand backpacks, and BPA-free water bottles, and the gear and clothing are well worn after many years of use—this is no fashion festival. There's no nail polish, no makeup, no hairdos. Several of the men are wearing Carhartt work pants, flannel shirts, and baseball caps; in fact, they're so uniformly gray-brown and rugged, nearly all bearded in salt-and-pepper, that, embarrassingly, out of the corner of my eye I often can't tell which one's my husband.

Even though I understand the PATC topo maps of this park—how each contour line represents one hundred feet of elevation change and thus determines exactly how steep the hike will be—I tend to gloss over this information and see the scene rather one-dimensionally. So even as we look across over the Shenandoah Valley from our high point on Skyline Drive and point "down there" as our destination, I do not have a good sense of the nature of our endeavor, especially given the initial hike description of it being easy, from the newsletter.

I am relishing the fact that I did not have to plan this hike, that others will be leading us, teaching us, and finding things for us, that I can simply look at what someone else will point out to me—a history-hike freeloader, for a change. I didn't bring a park map, historical land boundaries from when private individuals owned these lands, or notes from history books about the Shenandoah National Park story, and I have no idea whose former land we're on or whose former house we're going to visit. It is freeing, letting myself go in the hands of other experts to enjoy the park again as I once did, before I knew. On this glorious morning of clear air, away from my office job, I open myself up to experience whatever the universe will offer me.

Shenandoah, unlike national parks in the West, had little truly undisturbed wild country to preserve and protect when it was created. It had not really been wild since before the days of white-man discovery, iron smelting, and copper and manganese mining—or even before the Native Americans, who burned certain areas for balds. It had no "natural" state, exactly, to return to. The goal for the park has always been to restore, as close as possible, what it might have been like—or what it might have felt like—before Europeans arrived. From the 1930s to the 1980s, therefore, the philosophy of Shenandoah National Park, according to its supervisory biologist, Gordon Olson, was to "allow cultural features and values to fade away. There was no attention paid to them."

In the early decades, the park concentrated its efforts on visitor services—curating scenery, such as clearing the woods of dead chestnut trees. It built Skyline Drive and its overlook areas, stone guardrails, and drainage systems, and it replanted vegetation that had been disturbed—300,000 native trees and shrubs—and planted more than 5,000 new mountain laurels and other native plants. It developed the water, power, and communications infrastructure of the park. It used large, earthmoving machinery to build comfort stations, lodging, restaurants, parking lots, campgrounds, picnic areas, way stations, water fountains, and other structures for convenience and a not-too-wild experience. And, of course, it built trails: it converted the old roads into walking paths.

For former resident Melanchton Cliser, the memory of his life on the mountain didn't fade with these transformations and philosophies. He remained a thorn in the park administrators' side for the twelve years between his eviction in 1935 and his death at age seventy-four in 1947, writing to each new U.S. senator from Virginia and each new U.S. representative of his district, requesting additional money for his lost land, long after arbitration options—which he had never taken advantage of—had expired. Though even locals believed he received a hefty sum for his four and a half acres of commercial and residential property, he continually asked for more, and he never cashed the check for the $4,855 (or $83,100 in 2013) he received.

The memory didn't fade for former resident Richard Nicholson, either. He and other park residents wrote to U.S. Senator Harry F. Byrd in 1945 to inquire about reinhabiting their vacated homes, "on the grounds that the mountain people was badly misled when they sold their land for a park believing that they could stay there and not be forced to move." Byrd had the courtesy to forward these letters to and request comment from Harold L. Ickes, secretary of the interior, but Ickes's office responded that this action would be "unwarranted."

Though Lewis Willis of the Landowners Protective Association was allowed to stay on his land until he died, he continued working on resistance to the landtaking for more than twenty-five years.

In the 1960s, *Hollow Folk*—what former resident Murphy Nicholson called "filth and trash"—was republished. At the same time, Pollock's "highly self-serving and inaccurate" book, *Skyland*, was published as well. With these two acts, a revisionist history of the people of the park began to take place: one that "codified" the distorted idea of the lives of the mountain residents, seeing "subsistence agriculture—getting by rather than getting ahead—as backwards." According to a park historian, "the National Park Service came to accept [this history] as factual." These untruths became the source material for the park's visitor centers of that era—and are still used occasionally today at way stations operated by the park's concessionaire—and they restoked the flames of bigotry that raged for decades toward the mountain residents.

By the 1990s a woman named Lisa Berry decided to do something about it. While I was just discovering Shenandoah for the first time, splashing in swimming holes and camping at Naked Top or other locales, she was posting flyers in country stores and calling a meeting of a group she named Children of Shenandoah. Most of the people in attendance were not children at all, however, but rather people in their fifties, sixties, seventies, and beyond. They told stories of their lives and families on the mountain, showed each other old photographs, and wiped tears from their eyes.

"Part family reunion and part group therapy," this meeting was for attendees to talk about grief, anger, "burning shame," and also pride. Berry formed this group in May 1994 to preserve the heritage and culture of the people who once lived inside what is now the park—the life and times of a culture wiped off the map.

"A whole way of life was destroyed. They had their own culture, their own beliefs, their own codes, and now it's totally gone," Janis Shifflett Desaulniers, great-niece to Ambrose Shifflett and descendant of a large displaced family, told me. "I feel like an orphan."

Berry's primary goal was to work with park personnel to encourage them to present a more accurate history of the people of the park, as she considered the misinformation being presented to be "a slap in the face to people who had to watch as their homes burned down." She and her group hoped to correct printed brochures, information signs along Skyline Drive, as well as a video shown to millions of park visitors called *The Gift*, which perpetrated the idea of the property as a gift and depicted the mountain residents as poor, illiterate, filthy, barefoot hillbillies who raped the land with their industry (amid a backdrop of bluegrass banjo playing, of course). Never mind that many Americans suffered hardship during the Depression and that rural people everywhere made their living by farming, grazing, tanning, and timbering. Never mind that before the days of farmer-grazers, men were mining, making charcoal and pig iron, milling, and building roads throughout those mountains. Never mind that much of what made the lands seem raped, like the decimation of the American chestnut trees, the 1930s drought, and the construction of Skyline Drive itself, was out of these individuals' control.

The Children also wanted the park to memorialize their ancestors the way it did with the Civilian Conservation Corps boys, to build roads and walking paths to the abandoned backcountry cemeteries they wanted to visit, and to allow relatives of the interred to be admitted to the park for free. Some wanted to reclaim the families' old artifacts, which the park held in its possession; wanted them returned to their rightful owners just as Native Americans have lobbied for sacred items to be returned from museums. The park had catalogued 360,000 items—property records, personal histories, objects from homes—which were languishing, according to the Children, in boxes in various park buildings, collecting dust.

Some descendants had never seen any relics of their families' former lives in the mountains. "I have no way of knowing where my family's homes were," Desaulniers continued. "I know that's where my heritage is; I just don't know where. If I could find a piece of pottery," she said when I told her of my backcountry finds, "I would be beside myself."

According to the Children, it was time to "present the history of the park the way *we* know it happened and the way *they* know it happened."

It was time for a reckoning.

⟅⟆ Not even five minutes after dropping down from Skyline Drive through a cleared field and then onto the Appalachian Trail, we begin descending a rather precipitously steep, rocky, switchbacked old road, slippery with wet leaves, grown in with laurels and other brush, covered over in logs and branches, and narrower than any other old road I'd traveled in this park. In fact, this old road is in such a state of thick impassability that the group pretty much ignores the switchback turns and just heads straight down, road or no road, through the woods. All the while, this group of AARPers gab and laugh, completely unfazed and uninterrupted, while I—without walking pole, legs already turned to jelly from the steep and nearly uncontrolled downhill hike—cling to each branch or twig to keep my balance and prevent myself from tripping on one of the many obstacles or sliding down leaf-covered rocks to a painful landing.

Occasionally we stop for a nature break, and I don't mean a call-of-nature break, which no one ever seems to need. We are, I realize, among a group of nature nerds. We have Emily, a redheaded botanist who gets us talking about the sad fate of American chestnuts, which still attempt to grow in these types of forests, though the species has been pretty much decimated across its former range. This discussion commences an ongoing search for standing chestnuts, and along the way we witness many of considerable size that are beginning to show the telltale signs of disease. Anytime anyone in our group spots the fuzzy brown fruiting body of a chestnut on the ground ("But is it viable?" Emily always asks), the group gets into a frenzy trying to find the tree from whence the fruit came (a challenge because the trees are bare).

At one of our stops, after identifying the tree, Emily pulls out her special diameter tape and measures 6.5 inches. This collected information causes several people to jot down notes and make exclamations, though what it means in the grand scheme of things, I don't know; chestnuts are not sprouting any more successfully here than anywhere else in the East. At one instance, she points out grape fern and debates whether some unremarkable green stalks emerging from the ground are baby bluets, and the crowd circles around her, boasting about thus-and-such wildflowers seen last weekend, just before the first day of spring. There are, after all, more than seven hundred species of wildflowers here in this park. It's a nature-nerd competition of sorts: who can outdo the other by knowing more, being more engaged in nature in their daily lives, or being most interested.

Emily's friend Chip is a botanist too, particularly enamored with ferns, but today he seems fixated on determining if there are any red oaks in the park, a species especially difficult to identify because the bark is so variable on these trees and there isn't much else to go by. He shows the group cut-leaf toothwort and fumewort, two spring ephemerals. At one stop, he and Emily collect some flowering sedge from the base of a tree—illegal in a national park; they forget we're with a ranger—and they plan to identify it when they return home.

Then there's a quiet guy named Mike, an orchid and butterfly lover who shows me the leaves of the putty-root orchid poking out of the ground, while a woman I'll call Mary specializes in finding oak galls, golf-ball-sized encasements the tree creates on its leaves that surround wasp eggs. Nearly everyone in the group at one time or another wrinkles their noses and bad-mouths the spreading garlic mustard, an invasive, alien (and edible) weed that smells quite culinary.

Bob's a scat guy. He stops to show us bear poop, coyote dung, rabbit droppings, and other unnamed excrement, all of which he picks up with his bare hands. At our first such stop, he tells us about bears—how he believes Shenandoah National Park hosts more black bears per acre than any other national park. He handles the dried scat and points out the acorn remnants, a telltale sign that this is from last fall. He explains that one of the great highlights of a previous hike was finding a black bear's "fecal plug." During their winter inactivity, bears don't defecate at all, thanks in part to this handy piece of organic hardware they manufacture. When spring arrives, they push it out and resume their natural functions.

Everyone in the group is a generalized nature lover, and several people would fall into the category of hiking nut. Connie, who looks to be in her fifties and wears a day pack covered in various hiking-related patches, is an Appalachian Trail thru-hiker—someone who has hiked all 2,178 miles from Maine to Georgia in one three- to four-month trip. She also later became a high pointer, having ascended the highest peaks in forty-four states. She talks about these feats as if they are nothing. "Next time you are making plans somewhere, just see where the high point is, and do it on the way," she offers, though I have expressed no interest in this activity. Don and Elizabeth are quiet people; we hardly utter a word to one another the entire time. But they are Appalachian Trail thru-hikers as well; the fact that Elizabeth's trail name was Blister Sister tells me something about her experience.

Neil is a many-faceted nature nerd. Mostly he's a birder, logging every bird he sees or hears into eBird, a

Cornell University Lab of Ornithology–National Audubon Society website for data collection, as soon as we return home from an outing. Over the years, he has seen more than seventy species in Shenandoah, of the two hundred that reside or migrate here. He's also a reptile and amphibian aficionado, particularly into spotted salamanders, which he's been studying for more than fifteen years. A moment that would give him a lifetime high would be catching a glimpse of the elusive Shenandoah Salamander, an endangered species found only in a few locations in this park. Neil is a generalized vertebrate enthusiast as well—he dreams, more than anything else, about snakes.

Aside from Len, Jeremy, and Bob, who each feel different shades and varieties of interest, I seem to be the only one who really knows any of the details about the cultural history of the people of the park and the only one really fired up about the complicated brilliance and injustice of it all, how much the people suffered for our weekend zoological, botanical, and recreational pleasure. On this hike, I am thrilled to be the one to point out an old wash basin in a creek bed to several people I'm near, explaining that houses and barns once stood on this very land.

But all in all, when I assess the quirkiness and specialized interests of this group and I look at myself—lover of backcountry cemeteries, finder of off-trail house foundations and stone piles, seeker of graveyard myrtle and root cellars—I realize: these are people I understand. Even more so: these are the people of Shenandoah now.

～ When the park hired its first cultural resources manager in the 1990s, "its whole perspective changed," according to Olson. It began to conduct culturally appropriate research and analysis of the life and times of the mountain residents, to focus attention on a variety of historic structures that would become three hundred of those listed on the National Register of Historic Places, and, eventually, to survey and document the historic remnants of the people and their lost communities in a private database kept by the park. The park would employ geographic information systems, global positioning systems, photographs, maps, property assessment records, archeological investigations, and family histories to create the catalog, which is unavailable to the public.

"In 1945, assessments of the old log homes said they were worthless structures, with no value, no historic interest," recalled Steve Bair, the park's now-retired backcountry, wilderness, and trails manager, referring to such determinations as the opinion of a junior historian who was asked initially in 1935 and later in 1946 to assess the mountain residences to see what should be preserved and who came back saying nothing was especially unique or culturally distinctive. "Now, sixty-odd years later, we have a different attitude."

Most of the Children of Shenandoah's demands were not met, however. The park would never build a monument to the dispossessed, never release the objects it was cataloguing for a hard-to-access but professional permanent archive, and never build new roads to abandoned cemeteries. Some of the Children came around to seeing that opening up cemeteries to greater visitor access could lead to vandalism, and thus that issue died.

But the park made an about-face on many issues. It remade the video *The Gift*, retitling it *Shenandoah: The Gift* and no longer assigning blame to the mountain residents for callous exploitation of the land—resource extraction had been a common practice in an East Coast already denuded of pristine virgin forest—and presenting the lives of the residents in the context of the times. The film no longer suggests that the people gave their land as a donation or gift.

In the mid-1990s, the National Park Service collaborated with Colonial Williamsburg Foundation to conduct a "Survey of Rural Mountain Settlement" of Corbin, Weakley, and Nicholson Hollows, the archaeological findings of which disputed much of the misinformation about their life and times perpetrated by *Hollow Folk* and other sources.

The park and representatives from all eight counties that are part of the park also formed the Blue Ridge Committee for Shenandoah Park Relations to discuss problems, fears, and concerns that surface between the park and local communities. The group stemmed from landowners adjoining the park being opposed to the government ever trying to take more land (which happened in the 1960s to try to even out the jagged boundary), but it has evolved to cover topics such as how to deal with exotic, invasive plant species in the park; nearby dogs running loose; and other more mundane topics affecting park resources.

"There's not as much bad blood as there used to be," one committee member, who is on the board of supervisors in one of the counties and a descendant of the park, told me.

The park stacked the shelves of gift shops with books written by former park residents and their descendants about their lives on the mountain and populated its websites with stories and facts about the past. Above all, the park clearly gave the cultural resources manager and his staff "a seat at the table," according to Olson, involving them in decision making about the park at the highest levels.

Finally, with the Children of Shenandoah's participation, the modern-day park staff—a dream team of researchers, natural resource specialists, designers, and interpreters—redesigned the old visitors center exhibit, erecting a modern display that explains the range of resident demographics and the bitterness of the condemnations and all the trials and tribulations of what it took to make this park happen, the push and pull of dreams and determination on both sides. The team solicited and heeded comments and suggestions from descendants, local residents, and cultural sociologists for years, spending more than a million dollars and a decade in all for the permanent installation, which made its debut in 2006.

"My mantra has always been 'Honor the sacrifice,'" explained Claire Comer, one of the lead park employees on the project and a woman whose great-grandfather lost his vast summer grazing land to the park in the 1930s. In the exhibit, "nothing was sugarcoated. We told the story accurately and truthfully," she said, "and there was a lot of appreciation for that. I think the descendants feel that their concerns have been heard. What needed to happen was acknowledgement."

Part of the acknowledgment is this understanding, stated by the park's first employee, who only just recently passed away, someone who befriended many of the residents, someone with the perspective of the times' changing mores: "It isn't that they lost so much," Darwin Lambert said, "it's simply that somebody—against their will—shoved them. It's the resentment of somebody doing that to you. It's a violation of your pride and your independence. And they bitterly disliked that. And I don't blame them."

We continue downhill on what's supposed to be an old road but what seems like a truly tortuous and aimless bushwhack. It's so steep, I don't even let my mind wander to thoughts about coming back up. At one point we stop and Len points out what he's determined is the scene of the crime that inspired our hike, a completely random and unremarkable place in an ongoing grove of mountain laurels. The group pretty much shrugs and keeps going, and we never find the baby carriage. Steve, the park ranger, comments numerous times about signs of a new crime underway: freshly sheared-off limbs all along the route of this old road, which he says indicates poaching. Len later admits to me that it was he who cut those limbs, as he did a scouting and clearing run on this hike the weekend before and decided it was too grown in for passing.

Bob and his co-organizer Jane also tell me later that the hike was not what they expected, and they never would have rated it as easy. Jane, a salt-and-pepper-ponytailed woman who laughs a lot, keeps up a pretty rigorous and continuous stream of conversation with different folks, so that when I finally see the title on her baseball cap, "Trail Talker," I let out a good chuckle. (Technically, I learn later, this title refers to anyone who volunteers to chat up the Potomac Appalachian Trail Club at festivals and events.)

After about two and a half hours, we reach an old cabin, our destination for lunch. There's a crumbling stone chimney with a metal lintel, a rock foundation, and even several chestnut timbers still in place at the base, finely latticed and partially burnt from a lightning strike or wildfire. Inside the square outline of rocks, where I and a few others sit to eat our sandwiches—it just seems respectful to eat lunch inside the house—is a heap of rusty mattress springs.

The area is surrounded by numerous dry-stack rock walls and terracing. Nearby up the hill, daffodil greens have emerged. Don and Elizabeth, after a long search in the forest, finally materialize with a large, rusty metal coil, once used in a still to make moonshine, and the group goes nuts over it, everyone wanting to see it and snap a photo. (Then they return it to its forest home.)

No one knows who lived in this house, not even Len or Bob. Fellow hikers do not know what came before. To most of these überhikers and naturalists, the past is past—unknown, finished, and dead. Perhaps they never ran into an old cemetery in this park, or perhaps they did, perplexed. I didn't do my homework before this hike, didn't look up my maps and database, and so I sit in equal ignorance within the boundaries of this old home, feeling like a trespasser.

After lunch, Bob gives us a little nature talk about the power of the sun, how every seventeen degrees of its energy doubles the amount of insect activity. He also explains that the sun is what gets spring going in our area, warming the soil to its highest temperature all year, before the leaves come out and shade it. The group eats up these tidbits of knowledge—even Neil, who works as a teaching naturalist and is often the most knowledgeable nature guide on any hike.

Len doesn't appear to show enormous interest in the natural world, sometimes walking away and continuing to hike while we're gathered around a speaker like schoolchildren on a field trip, but he chimes in now, remembering one February "when all the spring peepers came out and had an orgy." He agrees with Bob in their need for the sun to give them energy, "because they can't afford to buy Viagra."

After the bit of dirty-old-man humor, Len turns around and leads us back up to the top. The hike up is relentlessly steep; we are no longer following an old road or a trail or any sign of clearing or civilization. We are simply scrambling on rocks, fumbling against gravity. In fact, we are hiking up fifteen hundred feet. "We could never lead a hike like this," Chip says excitedly, referring to the nature organization where he volunteers. "People would lodge complaints."

Halfway up, my legs are spent. It's not that this journey is particularly long; it certainly isn't the most arduous of bushwhacks I've done. But it's so staggeringly uphill, and these folks are relentless in their never-take-breaks mentality. Although I hike often, I sit at a desk all week and am used to stopping for long breaks when the going gets tough on the trail. Not this group. It is seemingly only for me that they pause and rest, standing all the while as I sit and recover my breath on a cold rock. I am awed, inspired, and crushed when I think of the age and vigor of this group and my inability to keep up with them.

But then later, when I need it most, they stop again for scat. The group tries to correlate the size of the numerous types of turds to the size of the species and whether an individual animal's size would affect its excretion dimensions. Bob explains that some animals, like rabbits, eat their excrement to absorb more nutrients. Neil chimes in that foxes like to display their goods on top of rocks and logs as territory markers. The group asks questions; some take notes. None of this talk grosses anyone out. And when everyone is finished pondering the nature of nature, in this—the most visited national park in the country when it opened in 1936—Len plods on, never losing a breath, to the final ascent.

This is just one hike of many this week for him and others, whose enthusiasm for the tiny wonders of life throughout these woods is too great to be contained in any assumption or stereotype. This handful of park visitors—a microcosm of all, members of the all-volunteer club that's been building trails in this park since before Shenandoah was even a park and renovating the mountain homes of former mountain residents since the families took their leave—enjoys the treasures of this park passionately, this land of biological abundance and refuge.

Former residents and their descendants knew the majestic beauty here too—"We discovered it first," descendant Ruth Kiger says with a smile.

I must admit, if I reconcile all the years I have hiked and camped and backpacked and bushwhacked and swam and frolicked in this park, all the weekends away from the rest of the world, finding pink lady's slipper orchids and wild azaleas and old apple butter kettles in the woods, all the adult years of my life when I became the person I am, with this place as integral as blood, with friends and family and my dear husband, who introduced me to the wild, it almost seems that the long, hard, eternal price for it all was worth it.

Acknowledgments

THIS BOOK IS NOT intended to be a complete history of the development of Shenandoah National Park. It is a summary, really, and my own story of discovery—just one contribution in a trove of existing books about the park's origins and the continuation of an ongoing dialogue. Historians, scholars, archaeologists, cultural resource specialists, former residents, park employees, and others have written serious histories, scholarly books, academic papers, magazine and journal articles, personal narratives, children's books, and other materials about the Shenandoah National Park story over several decades. One book could not possibly cover all the details or people involved in correspondence, events, and milestones over the course of the Shenandoah saga. In addition, researchers and leading thinkers have covered many of the broader related topics such as the nation's changing perspectives on wilderness and wild lands and the government's conservation-through-land-acquisition approach that emerged in the early twentieth century.

In regard to referring to living and historic figures by first or last names, I wish to acknowledge that I chose to refer to characters in the book formally or informally based on issues of writing clarity, the nature of the reporting in each instance, and the level of my feeling of familiarity with the person—real or imagined.

People from all parts of my life have generously given me their time and advice and expertise over many years while I worked on this book. I am grateful to all.

I thank current and former Shenandoah National Park personnel who answered many questions and assisted me with research: Steve Bair, Claire Comer, Karen Beck-Herzog, Dan Hurlburt, Kandace Muller, Gordon Olson, and others.

I give grateful acknowledgement to the following libraries and staff: the Arlington County, Virginia public library system; the Carrier Library's Special Collections at James Madison University; the Shenandoah National Park Archives; the Library of Virginia; the Smithsonian Archives; the Warren Heritage Society; the Rappahannock Historical Society; the National Archives; the University of Virginia's Albert and Shirley Small Special Collections Library; and the Library of Congress. I also thank the Potomac Appalachian Trail Club for its resources and help as well as my friend Jonathan Harmon, for lending me his Shenandoah-related library, and my friend Cyna Rosenthal, for helping me to interpret legal documents.

I appreciate the help of Mike Breeden, Tom and Kathy Conkey, Martha Davidson, Bart Frazier, Paul C. Hackley, Jurretta Jordan Heckscher, John F. Horan Jr., Kaye and Rick Kohler, Lyle W. Konigsberg, and the late Carolyn Reeder.

I am grateful to Kurt Rheinheimer for his encouragement of my writing and for his and Cara Ellen Modisett's decision to publish excerpts of my book in *Blue Ridge Country*.

I give immense thanks to the late Leonard F. Wheat for inspiring me to take bushwhacking to a new level, for answering numerous questions over the years, for providing bushwhacking directions to hidden park sites, for taking me to hidden places, and for conducting a keen editorial review of my manuscript. For Len's knowledge of this park, I consider him a national treasure.

I thank brothers Jeremy and Mike Ervin for many winter weekends of fun and "research," poking around the woods of Shenandoah National Park. I could never have imagined being so fortunate as to have found such sweet, kind, and eager bushwhacking buddies.

For the encouragement and nuts-and-bolts information on how to write a book and get it published, I owe much gratitude to my former instructors and current friends and colleagues at the Johns Hopkins University Master of Arts in Writing Program, especially Bill Loizeaux, Ed Perlman, and Tim Wendel. Also thank you to fellow Hopkins grads Sheryl Modlin and Herta Feely, for coaching. In addition, I am awed and inspired by the wisdom of my 2010 George Washington University intern, Elisa Valero, whose editorial and research assistance was invaluable.

Many thanks also to my other writer and nonwriter friends, who read and edited drafts, gave me contacts, and served as my cheerleaders, including Marilyn Bousquin, Rose Fitzpatrick, Diana Friedman, Katie Githens, Laura Long, Victoria Ludwig, Laurie McClellan, Leslie Mead, Anne Merrill, Elizabeth O'Neill, Karen Richardson, Craig Schultz, Karen Sosnoski, and many others too numerous to name.

Many Blue Ridge Mountain residents and their descendants kindly and generously shared family stories with me, and I am honored and humbled and so grateful to have made their acquaintance: Wayne Baldwin, Beulah Bolen, Mary Bolen Burner, Jeff Corbin, Jean Morris, the late Julia Shiflett Crosswell, Janis Shifflett Desaulniers, Ruth Kiger, Kenneth and Anne Shifflet, Elisabeth and Jim Weakley, Leanna Atkins Whorton, and family members at the September 2009 Bolen Cemetery family reunion.

I am grateful to the Virginia Center for the Creative Arts, Ron Goldfarb, and the Robert and Aida Goldfarb Art Law Literary Fund for the gift of time, space, and financial support for my 2010 fellowship at beautiful Mount San Angelo.

I could never have completed this book without the love and support of my family, who always believe in me and are my biggest fans—Bernie and Marcine Eisenfeld, Sara Eisenfeld, and Bonnie Eisenfeld and the late Hal Lehman. I am so grateful for the tremendous gift of their extraordinary love. An extra-special thanks to Mom for her expert research help, for reading many, many drafts of this book, for being my "patron of the arts," and for introducing me to history during my childhood in Philadelphia.

I overflow with unspeakable gratitude for Kristen Elias Rowley, my editor at the University of Nebraska Press, who understood my vision for this book. I laud Kristen and the entire team at UNP, who handled this manuscript with great care.

Above all, I thank my husband, Neil Heinekamp—for agreeing to my alternative work arrangements to allow me to write; for reading and editing every draft; for listening to every new fact I learned about Shenandoah National Park over many years; for accompanying me on nearly all my history hikes, cabin trips, bushwhacks, and other adventures whenever I commanded it; for being the naturalist and interpreter for all our hikes and fostering my interest in the wild; and for inspiring me and supporting me every step of the way in the process of writing this book. I could never, ever have done it without you. Nor would I have wanted to.

A version of "Timber Hollow Tale" was originally published as "Bushwhacking through Shenandoah History," *Blue Ridge Country*, March/April 2010.

A version of "All Souls' Day" was originally published as "All Souls Day in Shenandoah National Park," *Blue Ridge Country*, May/June 2011.

A version of the prologue was originally published as "Life & Death Near Butterwood Branch," *Blue Ridge Country*, November/December 2013.

Notes

AUTHOR'S NOTE

xi **"Cemetery seeking"**: Lambert, *Undying Past of Shenandoah National Park*, 275.

PROLOGUE

xiv **"They were some of the best days"**: LeRoy Nicholson, interview.

xvi **"has done more for the State"**: Horan, "Will Carson and the Virginia Conservation Commission" (1977), 123.

xvi **"a depth of vision"**: quoted in Horan, "Will Carson and the Virginia Conservation Commission" (1977), 208.

ALL SOULS' DAY

3 **"we will assume it is an obligation"**: U.S. Department of the Interior, National Park Service, Park Directive No. 90-38, see especially "Background."

4 **"to assume the full responsibility"**: U.S. Department of the Interior, National Park Service, Park Directive No. 90-38, see especially "Background."

5 **"natural vegetative succession"**: U.S. Department of the Interior, National Park Service, Park Directive No. 90-38.

5 **"receives the most attention"**: Shenandoah National Park, "Information on Known Cemeteries."

6 **"$500 at that time"**: Wood, interview.

A CABIN IN THE WOODS

15 **"son of a gun place"**: quoted in Floyd, *Lost Trails and Forgotten People*, 102.

19 **"Harvey's Special"**: quoted in Floyd, *Lost Trails and Forgotten People*, 93.

26 **"the park has received"**: quoted in Dudley, "Forestry Notes," 175.

26 "one committed, passionate, pain-in-the-ass": quoted in Goldberger, "Face-Lift," 23.

27 "human whirlwind": Shankland, *Steve Mather of the National Parks*, 56.

30 "You could go to Jones Mountain": quoted in Floyd, *Lost Trails and Forgotten People*, 103.

31 "A national park near the nation's capital": Northern Virginia Park Association, "National Park near the Nation's Capital."

31 some believed organized themselves: Lambert, *Undying Past of Shenandoah National Park*, 204.

31 "the sum total of new wealth": Allen to Zerkel, September 30, 1924.

31 "One fire will ruin a man": quoted in Floyd, *Lost Trails and Forgotten People*, 102.

32 "a terrible night": quoted in Floyd, *Lost Trails and Forgotten People*, 105.

32 "the most unique resort": Pollock, Skyland letterhead.

32 "the only dude ranch": Skyland, "Skyland."

33 "absolutely free": SANPC, "Answer to Government Questionnaire."

33 "There are within this area": SANPC, "Answer to Government Questionnaire."

34 "the matter of moving the people": Showalter to Byrd, December 2, 1926.

35 "If you take this place": quoted in Floyd, *Lost Trails and Forgotten People*, 112.

BUSHWHACK

40 "Once around the side": quoted in Shifflet, *Of Time and Place*, 107.

41 "They'd clear out a big room": Yager, interview.

42 "experienced, well-conditioned hiker": Wheat, *18 Cabins of Old Rag*, 5.

43 "Men over 60 years old"; "Grazing land owners": Amiss, "Minutes of Meeting of State Conservation and Development Commission."

47 "Oh, I'd love to"; "I couldn't walk up that mountain": Yager, interview.

47 "Go uphill along the E rim": Wheat, *18 Cabins of Old Rag*, 16.

49 "using Virginia's past": Horan, "Will Carson and the Virginia Conservation Commission" (1977), 15.

49 "A satisfied visitor": quoted in Horan, "Will Carson and the Virginia Conservation Commission" (1977), 17.

50 "There is no higher conception": Carson to Dodson, May 11, 1926.

51 "If a bomb had been exploded": quoted in Horan, "Will Carson and the Virginia Conservation Commission" (1977), 44.

51 some of the most important beef-producing: Lambert, *Undying Past*, 137.

51 "We must cut our cloth": Carson to Owners in Park Area, July 25, 1932.

52 "The commission has attached": "Park Land Owners View Expressed by Mr. Shifflett."

52 "quick and speedy": Carson to Byrd and Wortham, Fishburn, Dodson, Roberts, Farrar, Long, and Fippin, December 20, 1927.

52 "There will be no persuasion": Carson to Dodson, March 19, 1930.

52 "cold business matter": Carson to Dodson, March 19, 1930.

53 "a jigsaw puzzle": quoted in Lambert, *Administrative History*, 86.

53 "fish skeleton": quoted in Lambert, *Administrative History*, 96.

57 "The work up to this time": Carson to Wortham, Fishburn, Dodson, Roberts, Farrar, and Long, March 14, 1928.

58 "It was manifestly hopeless": quoted in Gilliam and Thomas, "Shenandoah National Park."

58 dignity was one of Virginia's greatest assets: Horan, "Will Carson and the Virginia Conservation Commission" (1984), 394.

58 "Them people lived good": Yager, interview.

HOLLOW FOLK HOLLOW

60 "The depths of ignorance": Henry, "In the Blue Ridge Hollows."

60 "Hidden communities of backward, illiterate": Henry, "Poor Whites Hem in Hoover's Camp."

60 "The basic fault lies": Henry, "In the Blue Ridge Hollows."

60 "under conditions close to": Sherman and Henry, *Hollow Folk*, v.

61 "a progressive school in a modern building": Sherman and Henry, *Hollow Folk*, 8.

61 "cleaner and better dressed": Sherman and Henry, *Hollow Folk*, 7.

61 "agriculture is organized": Sherman and Henry, *Hollow Folk*, 6.

61 "a few men are literate": Sherman and Henry, *Hollow Folk*, 6.

61 "at the lowest level": Sherman and Henry, *Hollow Folk*, 5.

62 "strange stories told": Poe, "A Tale of the Ragged Mountain."

62 "a haunted valley": Sherman and Henry, *Hollow Folk*, 81.

62 "At all hours the forms of nature": Sherman and Henry, *Hollow Folk*, 81.

63 "without bias"; "a leprous spot on our national body": quoted in Whisnant, Whisnant, and Silver, *Shenandoah National Park Official Handbook*, 139.

63 "liv[e] in what is": Warren, "Mountain Folk Know Nothing of Our Age."

63 "have emerged from the backwash of Time": Sherman and Henry, *Hollow Folk*, 79.

63 "the school has instilled in the children": Sizer to Bohn, September 13, 1928.

63 "might stir up a whole lot": Secretary to Cammerer, U.S. Department of the Interior, National Park Service, to Carson, September 21, 1928.

64 "These mountaineers have aptly been called": Sizer to Bohn, September 13, 1928.

64 "uncouth"; "a ragged, begrimed, vermin-infested": quoted in Horning, *In the Shadow of Ragged Mountain*, 10.

65 "I knew that without actually visiting": quoted in Horning, *In the Shadow of Ragged Mountain*, 61.

65 Some believe Pollock: Horning, *In the Shadow of Ragged Mountain*, 61.

65 "those of Corbin Hollow": quoted in Horning, *In the Shadow of Ragged Mountain*, 60.

67 "ghostly trunks of dead chestnuts": Sherman and Henry, *Hollow Folk*, 5.

71 "The first of these articles was read": "Writer on Park Draws on His Imagination."

71 "As a rule, the people living": "Writer on Park Draws on His Imagination."

74 "We didn't raise too much": Dodson, interview.

77 "lived a simple, uncomplicated life": Nicholson to President, Thomas S. Crowell Company, December 5, 1975.

77 "Our colleges are turning out": Nicholson to President, Thomas S. Crowell Company, December 5, 1975.

STRANDED

79 "He tried to dig out": Lambert, *Administrative History*, 141.

91 **"We are willing to make"**: quoted in Lambert, *Administrative History*, 90.

92 **"Landowners are informed"**: Willis, "First Chapter of the Sequel to the Shenandoah National Park Project."

92 **"The fundamental principles"**: Cliser, "Mr. Cliser Says the Republicans Are as Deep in the Mud as the Democrats Are in the Mire."

93 **"often a mere cross ridge"**: Zerkel to Carson, December 11, 1933.

93 **"If somebody had shot"**: Lambert, *Undying Past of Shenandoah National Park*, 230.

93 **"It will virtually destroy"**: W. C. Walton to President Roosevelt, February 10, 1934.

94 **"hallowed grounds"**: J. Via, response to thread.

95 **"King of Sugar Hollow"**: Lambert, *Undying Past of Shenandoah National Park*, 235.

96 **"Have you had your breakfast yet?"**: quoted in Yingst, "Taking of Via Mountain."

96 **"If you're my friend"**: Wood, interview.

97 **"hard as bullets"**: A. P. Walton to Mrs. Franklin D. Roosevelt, February 10, 1934.

100 **"like the English did"**: Wood, interview.

102 **"10 poles past grave-yard"**: Circuit Court of Albemarle County, Deed Book 152, p. 292.

LOST AND FOUND IN SHIFLET COUNTRY

108 **"quite far down"**: Lambert, *Undying Past of Shenandoah National Park*, 284.

110 **"residents will not be molested"**: quoted in Lambert, *Administrative History*, 224.

110 **"most humane undertakings"**: Carson to Wortham, Fishburn, Dodson, Booker, Farrar, Long, and Gilliam, June 15, 1934.

110 **"ruthless methods should be avoided"**: Davidson, "Shenandoah National Park—Its Genesis and Development."

110 **"every consideration of humanity"**: State Commission on Conservation and Development, November 2 press release.

110 **"no inhabitant need suffer"**: State Commission on Conservation and Development, November 2 press release.

110 **"this wholesale depopulation"**: Neve to the Secretary of the Interior, March 20, 1934.

112 **"I do not care to sell"**: quoted in Anne Frysinger Shifflet, *Of Time and Place*, 117.

112 **"I am sixty-four years old"**: quoted in Anne Frysinger Shifflet, *Of Time and Place*, 120.

113 **"Mom hated"**: quoted in Anne Frysinger Shifflet, *Of Time and Place*, 124.

113 **surely if he did**: Zerkel to Freeland, April 7, 1947; and Carolyn Reeder, "Cliser Eviction Story."

113 **"stood proudly in handcuffs"**: Dean, "Appalachian Trail of Tears."

114 **"My father believed"**: Reeder, "Cliser Eviction Story."

114 **"the impossible park"**: Lambert, *Undying Past of Shenandoah National Park*, 208.

A ROOM AT KILLAHEVLIN

118 **"a man of vision"**: quoted in Horan, "Will Carson and the Virginia Conservation Commission" (1977), 206.

118 **"amazing drive and resourcefulness"**: quoted in Horan, "Will Carson and the Virginia Conservation Commission" (1977), 207.

118 **"a pioneer"**: quoted in Horan, "Will Carson and the Virginia Conservation Commission" (1977), 207.

118 **"dazzling imaginative power"**: quoted in Horan, "Will Carson and the Virginia Conservation Commission" (1977), 207.

118 **"unselfish service"**: quoted in Carson files, LVH 0880, WHS.

121 **"Quitting never accomplishes anything"**: quoted in Horan, "Will Carson and the Virginia Conservation Commission" (1977), 139.

122 **"[Fishing] is a constant reminder"**: Hoover, "Address at Madison Courthouse," 228.

122 **"used all the arguments"**: Amiss, note in scrapbook.

122 **"the greatest single feature"**: quoted in Engle, "Greatest Single Feature."

122 **"I think everybody ought to"**: quoted in Lambert, *Herbert Hoover's Hideaway*, 56.

122 **"talk it over with Carson"**: quoted in Lambert, *Herbert Hoover's Hideaway*, 56.

122 **"matchless scenic wonders"; "mak[es] pictures"**: State Commission on Conservation and Development, November 16 press release.

123 **"Your commission has helped"**: State Commission on Conservation and Development, December 8 press release.

123 **"This awful Shenandoah National Park"**: Carson to Dodson, April 17, 1934.

123 **"a disagreeable and abhorrent"**: quoted in Gilliam and Thomas, "Shenandoah National Park."

123 **"eight weary years"**: quoted in Simmons, "Creation of Shenandoah National Park," 151.

123 **"Only the strictest sense"**: quoted in Horan, "Will Carson and the Virginia Conservation Commission, 1926–1934" (1984), 402.

124 **"We must aim at a real park"**: Cammerer to Carson, January 15, 1934.

124 **"scum"**: quoted in Gregg, *Managing the Mountains*, 126.

124 **"It is not very good faith"**: Carson to Cammerer, January 10, 1934.

124 **"We have quite a responsibility"**: quoted in Simmons, "Creation of Shenandoah National Park," 69.

124 **"very difficult problem"**: Carson to Wortham, Fishburn, Dodson, Booker, Farrar, Long, and Gilliam, June 15, 1934.

125 **"Resistance was encountered"**: quoted in Gilliam and Thomas, "Shenandoah National Park."

125 **"ruinous values"**: Willis, "Concerning the Landowners in the Proposed Park Area."

125 **"Neither I nor the State"**: Carson to Owners in Park Area, July 25, 1932.

125 **"Incredible as it may appear"**: "$900,000 Goes Begging for Somebody to Take It."

126 **"May it not be"**: Sizer, "Shenandoah National Park Area Notes on County Government—Madison Co."

126 **"To go through"**: quoted in Lambert, *Administrative History*, 224.

126 **"And neither you nor I"**: Carson to Wortham, Fishburn, Dodson, Booker, Farrar, Long, and Gilliam, April 13, 1934.

127 **"left to mold away"**: Steere, Steere Report.

127 **"very lightly put up"**: quoted in Konigsberg, "Nicholsons of Nicholson Hollow, Virginia," 91.

128 **"Do you think I am going to hate"**: quoted in Cowden-Brown, "Stories I Remember about the People Who Were Moved out of Their Homes to Make Shenandoah National Park Possible."

128 **"more alien than Mars"**: Dean, "Appalachian Trail of Tears."

128 **"for the purpose of inducing"**: Carson to Cammerer, January 10, 1934.

129 **"Near-chaos"**: quoted in Lambert, *Administrative History*, 228.

129 **"United only in their failure"**: Heckscher, "Blue Ridge Exile."

131 **"You have not co-operated"**: quoted in Powell, *Anguish of Displacement*, 43.

131 **"If you do not change your attitude"**: quoted in Powell, *Anguish of Displacement*, 52.

131 **"We have already done much more work"**: quoted in Lambert, *Administrative History*, 243.

131 **"I regard [the man] as a square-shooter"**: quoted in Powell, *Anguish of Displacement*, 76.

132 **"I have to observe the rules"**: Lassiter to Shifflett, April 3, 1936.

132 **"entirely nonpolitical"**: quoted in Horan, "Will Carson and the Virginia Conservation Commission" (1977), 122.

132 **"obviously and conspicuously"**: quoted in Horan, "Will Carson and the Virginia Conservation Commission" (1977), 199.

133 **"honorably relieve me of work"**: quoted in Horan, "Will Carson and the Virginia Conservation Commission" (1977), 119.

133 **"nauseating"**: Carson to Snead, September 20, 1934.

133 **"a last resort"**: quoted in Lambert, *Administrative History*, 136.

133 **"refused all efforts"**: quoted in Lambert, *Administrative History*, 137.

133 **"ground for a national park"**: Chiles to the President, March 23, 1937.

134 **"can hardly be justified"**: Chiles to Demaray, April 20, 1937.

134 **"feel very bad to leave"**: Draucker to Mrs. Franklin Roosevelt, September 17, 1936.

134 **"acts of unkindness"**: Chiles to the President, March 23, 1937.

134 **"was painful to both"**: "Charlottesville Officials Await Shenandoah Park Eviction Orders."

134 **"Who wrote this sob-story stuff?"**: Copy of handwritten note attached to Associated Press, "Ten in Family, 3 Ill, Evicted from Shenandoah Park Home."

134 **"the fundamental and basic facts"**: Brooks, "Memorandum for Mr. Cammerer from Brooks, August 22, 1932."

135 **"Sheriff . . . has just called this office"**: Hall to Cammerer, December 5, 1935.

137 **"Young 'Billy' Carson"**: "Death Strikes Hard Blow."

138 **"Enclosed herewith you will find"**: Carson to Cammerer, December 14, 1934.

139 **"The quality of mercy"**: Carson to Cammerer, December 14, 1934.

140 **"private occupancy of the lands"**: Chapman to Byrd, August 31, 1945.

140 **"meritorious"**: quoted in Lambert, *Administrative History*, 238.

140 **"as a matter of personal merit"**: Stephen to Hoskins, October 6, 1936.

140 "above average": Stephen to Hoskins, October 6, 1936.

140 "very good people": Stephen to Hoskins, October 6, 1936.

140 "crippled but . . . decent"; "excellent citizens,"; "really desirable and deserving": Stephen to Hoskins, October 6, 1936.

140 "With so distinguished a family record": National Society of U.S. Daughters of 1812, letter.

141 "just as humble as we could be": quoted in Moore, "Last of the Shenandoah Settlers."

141 a handwritten note on an old letter: See Cammerer to Carson, January 14, 1936.

142 "work of conservation,"; "recreation and re-creation": Roosevelt, "Address at the Dedication of Shenandoah National Park," 236.

142 "All across the Nation": Roosevelt, "Address at the Dedication of Shenandoah National Park," 237.

142 "a political pariah": Horan, "Will Carson and the Virginia Conservation Commission" (1977), 202.

143 "The establishment of Shenandoah": Byrd, "Statement by Senator Harry F. Byrd."

TIMBER HOLLOW TALE

146 "The murderer then dragged": Pollock, Skyland, 151.

149 "on the grounds that": Richard Nicholson to Byrd, August 7, 1945.

149 "unwarranted": Chapman to Byrd, August 31, 1945.

149 "filth and trash": Murphy Nicholson to President, Thomas S. Crowell Company, December 5, 1975.

149 "highly self-serving": Engle, "An Abused Landscape."

149 "codified": Engle, "An Abused Landscape."

149 "subsistence agriculture—getting by": Martin-Perdue, "Clouds Over the Blue Ridge," 62.

149 "National Park Service came to accept": Engle, "An Abused Landscape."

150 "Part family reunion and part group therapy": Dean, "Appalachian Trail of Tears."

150 "burning shame": Dean, "Appalachian Trail of Tears."

150 "a slap in the face": quoted in "Park Should Include All Parts of Story."

152 "present the history of the park": quoted in Gentry, "New Group Questions Park History."

158 "It isn't that they lost so much": quoted in Dean, "Appalachian Trail of Tears."

Bibliography

ARCHIVES

CCAC   Circuit Court of Albemarle County, Charlottesville VA.

CHC   Christine Hoepfner Collection, Carrier Library, Special Collections, James Madison University, Harrisonburg VA.

EGD   E. Griffith Dodson Papers, 1923–1962. Personal Papers Collection. Library of Virginia, Richmond VA.

EP   Executive Papers of Virginia Governor Harry F. Byrd, 1926–1930. State Government Records Collection. Library of Virginia, Richmond VA.

LFZ   L. Ferdinand Zerkel Papers, 1889–1962 [1924–1940]. Shenandoah National Park Archives, Luray VA.

NARA   National Archives and Records Administration, Records of the National Park Service, Central Classified Files, College Park MD.

OHC   Shenandoah National Park Oral History Collection, Carrier Library, Special Collections, James Madison University, Harrisonburg VA.

PHFB   Papers of Harry Flood Byrd Sr., Special Collections, University of Virginia Library, Charlottesville VA.

RMR   Shenandoah National Park Resource Management Records, 1926–1950. Shenandoah National Park Archives, Luray VA.

SCCD   State Commission on Conservation and Development Land Records, 1869–1995. Shenandoah National Park Archives, Luray VA.

TRH   Thomas R. Henry Papers, 1933–1967, Smithsonian Institution Archives, Washington DC.

WEC   William E. Carson. Scrapbooks, 1928–1941. Personal Papers Collection, Library of Virginia, Richmond VA.

WHS   Warren Heritage Society, Carson Files, Front Royal VA.

Adams, David A. *Renewable Resource Policy: The Legal and Institutional Foundations.* Washington DC: Island Press, 1993.

Albright, Horace M. *National Park Service: The Story Behind the Scenery.* Wickenburg AZ: KC Publications, 1987.

Allen, Harold, to Mr. L. Ferdinand Zerkel. September 30, 1924. LFZ 21205, series 1, box 1, folder 2.

"Americana: Parks but No Beef." *Pathfinder,* June 12, 1944.

Amiss, Fred T. "Minutes of Meeting of State Conservation and Development Commission, Capitol Building, Richmond." December 16, 1926. EP, accession 22561.

———. Note in scrapbook. WEC, accession 30463.

Anonymous. "#41–Via, Robert H." Survey form. N.d. SCCD 21203, box 8, folder 11.

———. "#183-Cliser, H. M." Land assessment. N.d. SCCD 21203, box 49, folder 14.

———. "Data concerning H. M. Cliser." N.d. RMR 21206, box 96, folder 37.

———. "Improvement Inventory," for Tract No. 41, owned by Robert H. Via. N.d. SCCD 21203, box 8, folder 11.

Associated Press. "Ten in Family, 3 Ill, Evicted from Shenandoah Park Home." March 21, 1937. CHC, SC 4042, box 2, folder 2.

Bair, Steve (Shenandoah National Park). Email correspondence with the author. January 22, 2010.

———. Telephone interview with the author. May 18, 2010.

Baldwin, Wayne. "An Account of the Bolen Family." Brochure. April 13, 2002.

———. "The Bolen Cemetery: Your Key to Understanding Family Connections of Those Buried Here." Brochure. N.d.

———. Email correspondence with the author. February 25, 2009; March 2, 2009; and May 21, 2010.

———. Interview with the author. September 12, 2009. Shenandoah National Park VA.

———. Telephone interview with the author. February 23, 2009.

Bashore, Henry W. *Old Rag Mountain: Rebirth of a Wilderness.* Heathsville VA: Northumberland Historical Press, 2006.

Beck-Herzog, Karen (Shenandoah National Park). Telephone interview with the author. May 14, 2010.

Bell, M. C., to Children of Shenandoah. October 23, 1981. CHC, SC 4042 box 2, folder 5.

Benchoff, H. J. *Report to Arno B. Cammerer, Director, National Park Service.* August 20, 1934. President, Shenandoah Valley, 1925–

33; and President, Shenandoah National Park Association, 1925. LFZ 21205, series 1, box 1, folder 6.

Bolen, Beulah. Interview with the author. September 12, 2009. Shenandoah National Park VA.

——. Telephone interview with the author. February 27, 2009.

Bowman, Rex. "Descendants Hope to Preserve Park's Past." *Charlottesville Daily Progress*, May 29, 1994. http://www.usgennet .org/usa/va/shenan/hope_to_preserve_park's_past.htm.

Breeden, M. (Blue Ridge Committee for Shenandoah Park Relations). Telephone interview with the author. May 14, 2010.

Brooks, Herbert. "Memorandum for Mr. Cammerer from Brooks, August 22, 1932." August 22, 1932. NARA, record group 79, central classified files, box 442.

Burner, Mary Bolen. Interview with the author. September 12, 2009. Shenandoah National Park VA.

Byrd, Harry, to the Honorable Harold L. Ickes. August 16, 1945. RMR 21206, box 98, folder 1.

Byrd, Harry F., Sr. "Statement by Senator Harry F. Byrd (D-VA) on the Death of William E. Carson, March 26, 1942." March 26, 1942. PHFB, accession 9700, 9700-B, box 400.

Cammerer, Arno B., to W. E. Carson. January 15, 1934. CHC, SC 4042, box 1, series 1, folder 4.

——, to W. E. Carson. January 14, 1936. CHC, SC 4042, box 1, folder 5.

Carson, W[illiam] E., to Governor H. F. Byrd and Coleman Wortham, Junius Fishburn, E. Griffith Dodson, Rufus Roberts, Thos. L. Farrar, Lee Long, and Elmer O. Fippin (members of the State Conservation and Development Commission). December 20, 1927. EGD, accession 25244.

——, to Hon. Arno B. Cammerer, January 9, 1934. CHC, SC 4042, box 1, series 1, folder 4.

——, to Hon. Arno B. Cammerer. January 10, 1934. CHC, SC 4042, box 1, series 1, folder 4.

——, to Hon. Arno B. Cammerer. January 16, 1934. CHC, SC 4042, box 1, series 1, folder 4.

——, to Hon. Arno B. Cammerer. January 26, 1934. CHC, SC 4042, box 1, series 1, folder 4.

——, to Hon. Arno B. Cammerer. December 14, 1934. CHC, SC 4042, box 1, folder 4.

——, to Mr. J. C. Carpenter Jr. September 22, 1934. EGD, accession 25244.

——, to Mr. E. G. Dodson. May 11, 1926. EGD, accession 25244.

——, to Mr. E. G. Dodson. March 19, 1930. EGD, accession 25244.

——, to Mr. E. Griffith Dodson. April 17, 1934. EGD, accession 25244.

——, to Hon. Junius Fishburn. March 23, 1934. EGD, accession 25244.

——, to Honorable Harold L. Ickes. January 26, 1934. CHC, SC 4042, box 1, series 1, folder 4.

——, to Owners in Park Area. July 25, 1932. Copy obtained from WHS visitor display.

——, to E. A. Snead, Esq. September 20, 1934. EGD, accession 25244.

——, to Messrs. Coleman Wortham, Junius P. Fishburn, E. G. Dodson, M. B. Booker, T. L. Farrar, Lee Long, and R. A. Gilliam (members of the State Commission on Conservation and Development) (regarding a letter sent to Secretary Ickes on April 12). April 13, 1934. EGD, accession 25244.

——, to Coleman Wortham, Junius P. Fishburn, E. Griffith Dodson, M. B. Booker, Tomas L. Farrar, Lee Long, and R. A. Gilliam (members of the State Commission on Conservation and Development). June 15, 1934. EGD, accession 25244.

——, to Coleman Wortham, Junius P. Fishburn, E. Griffith Dodson, Rufus G. Roberts, Thomas L. Farrar, and Lee Long (members of the State Conservation and Development Commission). March 14, 1928. EGD, accession 25244.

Chapman, Oscar, Assistant Secretary of the Department of the Interior, to Hon. Harry Byrd, U.S. Senate. August 31, 1945. RMR 21206, box 98, folder 1.

"Charlottesville Officials Await Shenandoah Park Eviction Orders." *Charlottesville Daily Progress*, December 5, 1935.

Children of Shenandoah. "Background." N.d. Attachment to "Cemetery Directive '97." Accessed January 2, 2014, http://www.usgennet.org/usa/va/shenan/cemetery_directive_'97.htm.

——. "Children of Shenandoah." Home page. Accessed January 2, 2014, http://www.usgennet.org/usa/va/shenan/index.htm.

Chiles, R. P., to A. F. Demaray, Department of the Interior. April 20, 1937. CHC, SC 4042, box 1, folder 7.

——, to the President. March 23, 1937. CHC, SC 4042, box 1, folder 7.

Circuit Court of Page County at Luray VA. Notice of Condemnation. *Page News and Courier* (Luray VA). September 2, 1930.

City Club. "Meeting of the SNP 'Nuts.'" March 6, 1925. SCCD 21203, box 1, folder 8.

Circuit Court of Albemarle County. Deed Book 152. CCAC. Charlottesville VA.

Circuit Court of Albemarle County. Deed Book 191. CCAC. Charlottesville VA.

Cliser, H. M. "Mr. Cliser Says the Republicans Are as Deep in the Mud as the Democrats Are in the Mire." *Page News and Courier* (Luray VA), October 25, 1929.

———. "Notice Warning." August 13, 1930. SCCD 21203, box 49, folder 14.

Comer, Claire (Shenandoah National Park). Telephone interview with the author. May 19, 2010.

Conkey, Tom (Killahevlin Bed and Breakfast). Interview with the author. January 8 and 9, 2012. Front Royal VA.

Conkey, Tom, and Kathy Conkey (Killahevlin Bed and Breakfast). Interview with the author. July 22, 2010. Front Royal VA.

Corbin, Jeff. Telephone interview and subsequent email communication with the author. January 22, 2010.

Corbin, Virgil F. "From a Primitive Life to Modern Living." N.d. OHC, SC 4030 [SdArch SNP], SNP-036, box Z.

———. Interview by Dorothy Noble Smith. January 3, 1979. OHC, SdArch SNP, SNP-36.

Cowden-Brown, Mozelle. "Stories I Remember about the People Who Were Moved out of Their Homes to Make Shenandoah National Park Possible." N.d. RMR 21206, box 99, folder 1.

Crosswell, Julia Shiflett. Telephone interview with the author. March 28, 2002.

Davidson, Arthur. "Shenandoah National Park—Its Genesis and Development." January 24, 1935. EGD, accession 25244.

Dean, Eddie. "Appalachian Trail of Tears." *Washington City Paper*, February 28–March 6, 1997. Accessed December 20, 2014, http://www.washingtoncitypaper.com/articles/12175/appalachian-trail-of-tears.

"Death Strikes Hard Blow." Obituary, *Daily Independent* (Winchester VA), January 19, 1925. Retrieved from Killahevlin private files.

Desaulniers, Janis Shifflett. Telephone interview with the author. April 3, 2008.

Dillard, Annie. *The Writing Life*. New York: Harper and Row, 1989.

Dodson, Estelle Nicholson. Interview by Dorothy Noble Smith. November 23, 1977. OHC, SdArch SNP, SNP-42.

Draucker, G., to Mrs. Franklin Roosevelt. September 17, 1936. CHC, SC 4042, box 1, folder 7.

Dudley, William R., ed. "Forestry Notes," *Sierra Club Bulletin* 4, no. 2 (1902): 173–76. http://books.google.com/books?id=jeERAAAAYAAJ&pg=PR2&lpg=PR2&dq=%22sierra+club+bulletin%22+%22forestry+notes%22+dudley+roosevelt+volume+4&source=bl&ots=HJvan2muk3&sig=l4UprBTigYdtWleVfNKvz-yImfM&hl=en&sa=X&ei=UWHHUo3AFcyukAeH3IDQCQ&ved=0CCkQ6AEwAA#v=onepage&q=%22sierra%20club%20bulletin%22%20%22forestry%20notes%22%20dudley%20roosevelt%20volume%204&f=false.

Duncan, Walter. Telephone interview with the author. August 4, 2010.

Dunn, Durwood. *Cades Cove: The Life and Death of a Southern Appalachian Community, 1818–1937*. Knoxville: University of Tennessee Press, 1988.

Dutton, Mrs. Ben B., Jr. Telephone interview with the author. September 2010.

Encyclopedia Virginia. "Relocation of Shenandoah Residents." August 2008. 6:45. Radio program from VFH Radio, a program of the Virginia Foundation of the Humanities. http://www.encyclopediavirginia.org/media_player?mets_filename=evm00000971mets.xml.

———. "William E. Carson (1870–1942)." Last modified November 23, 2010. http://www.encyclopediavirginia.org/Carson_William_Edward_1870-1942.

Engle, Reed. "An Abused Landscape." Shenandoah National Park. Last modified December 11, 2013. http://www.nps.gov/shen/historyculture/abused_landscape.htm.

———. "The Greatest Single Feature." Shenandoah National Park. Last modified December 11, 2013. http://www.nps.gov/shen/parknews/drive_75th_ann.htm.

———. *The Greatest Single Feature . . . A Sky-Line Drive*. Luray VA: Shenandoah National Park Association, 2006.

———. *In the Light of the Mountain Moon: An Illustrated History of Skyland*. Luray VA: Shenandoah National Park Association, 2003.

———. "Miriam M. Sizer: Patroness or Patronizing." Shenandoah National Park. Last modified December 11, 2013. http://www.nps.gov/shen/historyculture/miriamsizer.htm.

———. "Shenandoah: Laboratory for Change." CRM (*Cultural Resource Management*) 21, no. 1 (1998): 34–35.

———. "Shenandoah National Park Historical Overview." Shenandoah National Park. Last modified December 11, 2013. http://www.nps.gov/shen/historyculture/historicaloverview.htm.

Engle, Reed, and Caroline Janney. *A Database of Shenandoah National Park Land Records.* Luray VA: Shenandoah National Park Association, October 15, 1997.

Fievet, Charles J., Melanie L. Allen, and James R. Web. *Documentation of Landuse and Disturbance History in Fourteen Intensively Studied Watersheds in Shenandoah National Park, Virginia: 1920s to Present.* Charlottesville: Department of Environmental Sciences, University of Virginia, February 10, 2003.

Floyd, Tom. *Lost Trails and Forgotten People: The Story of Jones Mountain.* Vienna VA: Potomac Appalachian Trail Club, 2004.

Fowler, Tom. "Mrs. Shenk, 86, Is Last of Old 'Park Families.'" *Page News and Courier* (Luray VA), May 11, 1972.

Frenkiel, Susan. *American Chestnut: The Life, Death, and Rebirth of a Perfect Tree.* Berkeley: University of California Press, 2007.

Garvey, Edward B. "The Story of Corbin Cabin." Transcribed June 1962 by Potomac Appalachian Trail Club. Poster in Corbin Cabin, Shenandoah National Park; and RMR 21206, box 96, folder 45.

Gentry, Bill. "New Group Questions Park History." *Valley Banner* (Elkton VA), December 29, 1994.

Gilliam, George H., and William G. Thomas III. "Shenandoah National Park. In: New Deal Virginia: The Ground Beneath Our Feet—A Documentary Film Series and Website About Virginia's History After the Civil War; Episode 1: New Deal Virginia." N.d. Accessed June 18, 2009, http://www.vahistory.org/shenandoah.html (site discontinued).

Goldberger, Paul. "Face-Lift: The Falls." *New Yorker,* August 3, 2009.

Gregg, Sara M. *Managing the Mountains: Land Use Planning, the New Deal, and the Creation of a Federal Landscape in Appalachia.* New Haven CT: Yale University Press, 2010.

Hackley, Paul. *A Hiker's Guide to the Geology of Old Rag Mountain, Shenandoah National Park, Virginia.* Open-file report 00-263. Reston VA: U.S. Geological Survey, 2006. http://pubs.usgs.gov/of/2000/of00-263/of00-263.pdf.

Hall, Wilbur, Western Union telegram to Arno B. Cammerer. December 5, 1935. NARA, record group 79, central classified files, boxes 1654 and 610.

Heatwole, Henry. *Guide to Shenandoah National Park and Skyline Drive.* Luray VA: Shenandoah Natural History Association, 1997.

Heckscher, Jurretta Jordan. "Blue Ridge Exile: The Displacement of Mountain Residents in the Creation of Shenandoah National Park." Unpublished term paper, George Washington University, Spring 1990.

Henry, Thomas R. "In the Blue Ridge Hollows." *Washington Evening Star*, n.d. TRH, record unit 7347.

———. "Poor Whites Hem in Hoover's Camp." *Oregonian*, September 3, 1929.

Herndon, M. L. Membership application form. N.d. CHC, SC 4042, box 2, folder 5.

Hoover, Herbert. "Address at Madison Courthouse." In *The Height of Our Mountains*, edited by Michael P. Branch and Daniel J. Philippon, 227–28. Baltimore: Johns Hopkins University Press, 1998. Originally spoken on August 17, 1929.

Horan, John F., Jr. Email correspondence with the author. July 26, 2010.

———. "Will Carson and the Virginia Conservation Commission, 1926–1934." Master's thesis, University of North Carolina, Chapel Hill, 1977.

———. "Will Carson and the Virginia Conservation Commission, 1926–1934." *Virginia Magazine of History and Biography* 92, no. 4 (October 1984): 391–415.

Horning, Audrey. "The Displaced." Shenandoah National Park. Accessed January 3, 2014, http://www.nps.gov/shen/history culture/displaced.htm.

———. *In the Shadow of Ragged Mountain: Historical Archaeology of Nicholson, Corbin & Weakley Hollows*. Luray VA: Shenandoah National Park Association, 2004.

Howell, J. W., Sec. Treas. "Note for the files." December 21, 1950. RMR 21206, box 98, file 29.

Jones, R. B. (White Hall Hunt Club). Telephone interview with the author. December 2009.

Kiger, Ruth. Interview with the author. June 2010 and September 2010. Washington VA.

———. Telephone interview with the author. November 3, 2010.

Killahevlin Bed and Breakfast. "Killahevlin Bed and Breakfast." Home page. Accessed December 20, 2013, http://www.vairish .com/history.html.

Kilpatrick, Sharon. "Two Natives Share Memories of Mountain Hollows." *Rappahannock News*, December 9, 1992.

Konigsberg, Lyle W. "The Nicholsons of Nicholson Hollow, Virginia." Unpublished term paper, Fall 1979. RMR 21206, box 99, folder 4.

Laing, C., to Congressman Cantor. August 20, 2001. Children of Shenandoah. http://www.usgennet.org/usa/va/shenan /congressman_eric_cantor.htm.

Lambert, Darwin. *Administrative History: Shenandoah National Park, 1924–1976.* Luray VA: National Park Service, 1979. http://www.nps.gov/history/history/online_books/shen/admin.pdf.

———. *The Earth-Man Story: Parks, Man, and His Environment.* Jericho NY: Exposition Press, 1972.

———. *Herbert Hoover's Hideaway.* Luray VA: Shenandoah Natural History Association, 1971.

———. *The Undying Past of Shenandoah National Park.* Lanham MD: Roberts Rinehart, 1989.

Lassiter, J[ames] R., to Mr. Clark Shiflett. March 26, 1936. RMR 21206, box 98, folder 30.

———, to Mrs. Mitt Shifflett. April 3, 1936. RMR 21206, box 98, folder 30.

———. "Shenandoah National Park." *Commonwealth,* July 1936.

"Last Family Forcibly Ejected from Shenandoah Park Home." *Washington Evening Star,* March 21, 1937. CHC, SC 4042, box 2, folder 2.

Lippman, Thomas W. "Old-Timer Recalls 1st Eviction in '26," *Washington Post,* May 26, 1974.

Littlejohn, Margaret. *Shenandoah National Park Visitor Study, Summer 2001, Report 127.* Visitor Services Project, National Park Service, U.S. Department of Interior, April 2002.

Mackintosh, Barry. "The National Park Service: A Brief History." National Park Service. Last modified 1999. http://www.nps.gov/history/history/hisnps/NPSHistory/npshisto.htm.

Martin-Perdue, Nancy. "Clouds over the Blue Ridge." *Commonwealth,* May 1983.

Momaday, N. Scott. *The Way to Rainy Mountain.* Albuquerque: University of New Mexico Press, 1976.

Moody, Amanda. "Additional Information on the Via Family of Via Gap." Ca. 1976. RMR 21206, box 98, folder 49.

———. "Via Gap." Ca. 1976. RMR 21206, box 98, folder 49.

Moore, Irene. "Last of the Shenandoah Settlers." *American Forests,* February 1966.

Morris, Jean. Interview with the author. June 2010 and September 2010. Washington VA.

———. Telephone interview with the author. November 3, 2010.

"National Park Deeds Signed by Governor." *Richmond Times-Dispatch,* August 11, 1934. SCCD 21203, box 8, folder 12.

National Park Service. "Yellowstone National Park's First 130 Years." Yellowstone National Park. Accessed December 20, 2013, http://www.windowsintowonderland.org/history/army&nps/page11.htm.

National Society of United States Daughters of 1812. Letter. NARA, record group 79, central classified files, box 1654.

Neve, F. W., to the Secretary of the Interior. March 20, 1934. CHC, SC 4042, box 1, folder 7.

Nicholson, LeRoy. Interview by Dorothy Noble Smith. May 16, 1979. OHC, SdArch SNP, SNP-100.

Nicholson, Murphy, to President, Thomas S. Crowell Company. December 5, 1975. RMR 21206, box 99, folder 5.

Nicholson, Richard, to Mr. Harry F. Byrd. August 7, 1945. RMR 21206, box 98, folder 1.

"$900,000 Goes Begging for Somebody to Take It." *New York Times*, January 28, 1934. CHC, SC 4042, box 2, folder 2.

North Carolina State Archives. "Finding Aid of the Appalachian National Park Association: General Records, 1899–1936." Accessed January 12, 2014, http://ead.archives.ncdcr.gov/wra /org_anpa_general_records.xml.

Northern Virginia Park Association. "A National Park near the Nation's Capital." Information Bulletin, November 17, 1924. LFZ 21205, series 1, box 1, folder 4.

Nowak, Liesel. "Exhibit Explores Displaced Lives," *Charlottesville Daily Progress*, August 2, 2004.

Olson, Gordon (Shenandoah National Park). Telephone interview with the author. May 18, 2010.

O'Neill Knight, Theresa. "The Children of the Shenandoah Reclaim Their Heritage." *Culpeper News*, November 1996.

"Park Evictions up to Courts." *Charlottesville Daily Progress*, December 6, 1935.

"Park Land Owners View Expressed by Mr. Shifflett." *Page News and Courier* (Luray VA), May 12, 1931.

"Park Should Include All Parts of Story." *Charlottesville Daily Progress*, October 11, 1994.

Perdue, Charles L., Jr., and Nancy J. Martin-Perdue. "Appalachian Fables and Facts: A Case Study of the Shenandoah National Park Removals." In *Process, Policy, and Context: Contemporary Perspectives on Appalachian Culture*, edited by David E. Whisnant, 84–104. Boone NC: Appalachian State University, 1980.

Petty, M. Telephone interview with the author. July 28, 2009.

Poe, Edgar Allen. "A Tale of the Ragged Mountain." *Godey's Lady's Book*, March 1844.

Pollock, George Freeman. *Skyland: The Heart of the Shenandoah National Park*. Baltimore MD: Chesapeake Book Company, 1960.

———, Skyland letterhead. N.d. LFZ 21205, series 1, box 1, folder 4.

———, to Hon. Wm. E. Carson. November 20, 1930. CHC, SC 4042, box 1, folder 4.

Potomac Appalachian Trail Club. *Circuit Hikes in Shenandoah National Park*, 15th ed. Vienna VA: Potomac Appalachian Trail Club, 2005.

Powell, Katrina M. *The Anguish of Displacement: The Politics of Literacy in the Letters of Mountain Families in Shenandoah National Park*. Charlottesville: University of Virginia Press, 2007.

———. *Answer at Once: Letters of Mountain Families in Shenandoah National Park, 1934–1938*. Charlottesville: University of Virginia Press, 2009.

Pub. L. No. 69-268, Chap. 363, 44 Stat. 616 (May 22, 1926).

Reeder, Carolyn. "The Cliser Eviction Story." *Page News and Courier* (Luray VA), October 6, 1983.

Reeder, Carolyn, and Jack Reeder. *Shenandoah Heritage: The Story of the People before the Park*. Vienna VA: Potomac Appalachian Trail Club, 1978.

———. *Shenandoah Secrets: The Story of the Park's Hidden Past*. Vienna VA: Potomac Appalachian Trail Club, 1991.

Robert H. Via v. The State Commission on Conservation and Development of the State of Virginia. 296 U.S. 549 (1935).

Roosevelt, Franklin Delano. "Address at the Dedication of Shenandoah National Park." In *The Height of Our Mountains*, edited by Michael P. Branch and Daniel J. Philippon, 236–37. Baltimore: Johns Hopkins University Press, 1998. Originally spoken on July 3, 1936.

Runte, Alfred. *National Parks: The American Experience*. Lincoln: University of Nebraska Press, 1979.

SANPC (Southern Appalachian National Park Committee). *Answer to Government Questionnaire concerning Proposed Southern Appalachian National Park*, as filled out by George Freeman Pollock. N.d. Shenandoah National Park. http://www.nps.gov/shen/historyculture/upload/s.a.n.p.c._questionnaire.pdf.

Schullery, Paul. *Mountain Time: A Yellowstone Memoir*. Albuquerque: University of New Mexico Press, 2008.

Secretary to Mr. Cammerer, U.S. Department of the Interior, National Park Service, to Mr. W. E. Carson. September 21, 1928. CHC, SC 4042, box 2, folder 1.

Shankland, Robert. *Steve Mather of the National Parks*. New York: Alfred A. Knopf, 1951.

Shenandoah National Park, National Park Service. DVD of historical maps of property lines of all previous landowners in eight counties. Provided by Dan Hurlburt, Shenandoah National Park.

———. *The Gift.* VHS. Produced by Harpers Ferry Center. 1982. 20 min.

———. "Information on Known Cemeteries within Shenandoah NP." Memorandum to Superintendent, Shenandoah NP, from Chief Ranger, July 27, 1954. Accessed online at Shiflett Family Genealogy, "Historical and Human Interest," http://www .shiflett-klein.com/shifletfamily/HHI/Shen/shenpark2.html.

———. "Park Building Survey" for Cliser Farmstand. Steer Report No. 4. February 28, 1944. RMR 21206, box 97, folder 31.

———. Park Directive NCR-406: Cemetery Maintenance and Use. Referenced online by Children of Shenandoah. Last modified September 26, 2001. http://www.usgennet.org/usa/va/shenan /snp_cemetaries.htm.

———. *Shenandoah: The Gift.* DVD. Produced by Harpers Ferry Center. 2001. 15 min.

———. "Shenandoah National Park Visitor Statistics." Shenandoah National Park. Last modified 2006. http://www.nps.gov/shen /parkmgmt/upload/visitor_stats.pdf.

Sherman, Mandel, and Thomas R. Henry. *Hollow Folk.* Richmond: Virginia Book Company, 1933.

Shifflet, Anne Frysinger. Interview with the author. May 2, 2010. Shenandoah National Park VA.

———. *Of Time and Place: A Shifflett-Morris Saga.* Harrisonburg VA: published by author, 2002.

Shifflet, Kenneth. Interview with the author. May 2, 2010. Shenandoah National Park VA.

Showalter, W. J., to Honorable Harry F. Byrd. December 2, 1926. EP, accession 22561.

Shugard, Sharon. "Hot Springs National Park: A Brief History of the Park." National Park Service. Last modified November 2003. http://www.nps.gov/hosp/historyculture/upload/Brief %20history%20of%20bathhouse%20row.doc.

Simmons, Dennis E. "Conservation, Cooperation, and Controversy: The Establishment of Shenandoah National Park, 1924–1936." *Virginia Magazine of History and Biography* 89, no. 4 (1981): 387–404.

———. "The Creation of Shenandoah National Park and the Skyline Drive, 1924–1936." PhD diss., University of Virginia, 1978.

Singleton, Maura. "Oral Tradition Carries Sadder History of Shenandoah Park." *Charlottesville Daily Progress*, October 12, 1996.

Sizer, Miriam M. "Shenandoah National Park Area Notes on County Government—Madison Co." N.d. NARA, record group 79, central classified files, box 442.

——, to Mr. John Bohn, New York Times. September 13, 1928. CHC, SC 4042, box 2, folder 1.

Skyland. "Skyland." N.d. NARA, record group 79, central classified files, box 1682.

Smith, Leef. "Anger in Appalachia: Researchers Fighting to Open Records on 1930s Shenandoah Park Resettlement," *Washington Post*, March 6, 2000. Reprinted on the American Land Rights Association website.

Spence, Mark David. *Dispossessing the Wilderness*. Oxford: Oxford University Press, 1999.

State Commission on Conservation and Development. November 2 press release. EGD, accession 25244.

——. November 16 press release. EGD, accession 25244.

——. December 8 press release. EGD, accession 25244.

Steere, Edward. Steere Report, SNP-146, 2-12-44. 1944. Based on "Park Building Survey" for "Aaron Nicholson House" and "Russ Nicholson or John R. Nicholson House." RMR 21206, box 97, folders 58 and 66.

Stephen, H. T., to R. T. Hoskins, Chief Ranger, Department of Interior, National Park Service. October 6, 1936. CHC, SC 4042, box 1, folder 5.

Swift, William. "Stephen T. Mather: 1867–1930." National Park Service. Last modified December 1, 2000. http://www.nps .gov/history/history/online_books/sontag/mather.htm.

Taylor, Fionn. "Carbide Lighting System." Fionn.org. http://www .healeyhero.co.uk/rescue/glossary/carbide.htm.

Thomas Jackson Rudacille v. State Commission on Conservation and Development. 155 Va. 808, 156 S.E. 829 (1931).

"3 U.S. Judges Hear Park Case Today." *Harrisonburg Daily News-Record*, December 10, 1934.

U.S. Department of the Interior, National Park Service. Park Directive No. 90-38. Memorandum to all employees from superintendent. September 19, 1997. Accessed online at Children of Shenandoah, "Cemetery Directive '97," USGenNet, http://www.usgennet.org/usa/va/shenan/cemetery_directive '97.htm.

——. Statement of Significance. Skyline Drive Historic District. February 23, 2009. http://www.nps.gov/shen/historyculture /upload/nhl_skyline_drive_historic_district_final.pdf.

———. "Wilderness." National Park Service. http://wilderness.nps .gov/wilderness.cfm.

Via, J. Response to thread called, "Looking for information on Via Cemetery Shenandoah Park VA." RootsWeb. December 2, 2001. http://archiver.rootsweb.ancestry.com/th/read/VIA /2001-12/1007342261.

Via, L. Email correspondence with the author. March 2008.

Via vs. State Commission on Conservation and Development of State of Virginia. 9 F. Supp. 556 (W.D. Va. 1935).

Vintage Virginia Apples. "Albemarle Pippin." https://www.albemarle ciderworks.com/orchard/apple/albemarle-pippin.

Walton, A. P., to Mrs. Franklin D. Roosevelt. February 10, 1934. CHC, SC 4042, box 1, folder 7.

Walton, W. C., to President Roosevelt. February 10, 1934. Referenced in letter to Mrs. Franklin D. Roosevelt from A. P. Walton. CHC, SC 4042, box 1, folder 7.

Warren, Virginia Lee. "Mountain Folk Know Nothing of Our Age." Washington Post, November 3, 1935.

Weakley, Elisabeth. Telephone interview with the author. December 31, 2008, and May 22, 2013.

"W. E. Carson, Jr., 16, Dies at Home from Pneumonia." Obituary, January 19, 1925. Retrieved from Killahevlin private files.

Wheat, Leonard F. The 18 Cabins of Old Rag: A Field Guide for Bushwhackers. Vienna VA: Potomac Appalachian Trail Club, 1994.

———. Email correspondence with the author. 2009–2012.

Whisnant, Anne Mitchell. Super-Scenic Motorway: A Blue Ridge Parkway History. Chapel Hill: University of North Carolina Press, 2006.

Whisnant, Anne Mitchell, David E. Whisnant, and Tim Silver. Shenandoah National Park Official Handbook. Luray VA: Shenandoah National Park Association, 2011.

Whorton, L. A. Telephone interview with the author. September 24, 2009.

Wilhelm, Gene, Jr. "Shenandoah Resettlements." Pioneer America 14, no. 1 (1982): 15–40.

"William E. Carson: Cornelius Amory Pugsley Silver Medal Award, 1934." American Academy for Park and Recreation Administration. With contributions by Stephanie Yuill. http://www.aapra.org/Pugsley/CarsonWilliam.html.

Willis, Lewis. "Concerning the Landowners in the Proposed Park Area." Page News and Courier (Luray VA), June 28, 1932. CHC, SC 4042, box 2, folder 2.

———. "The First Chapter of the Sequel to the Shenandoah National Park Project." *Page News and Courier* (Luray VA), October 7, 1929. CHC, SC 4042, box 2, folder 2.

Wood, Ray. Interview by Amanda Moody. September 14, 1977. OHC, SdArch SNP, SNP-135.

Wright, Barbara. "Some there be which have no memorial." *VCCA Journal* 9, no. 1 (1994): 27–34.

"Writer on Park Draws on His Imagination." *Page News and Courier* (Luray VA), September 3, 1929.

Yager, Mattie. Interview by Dorothy Noble Smith. April 25, 1978. OHC, SdArch SNP, SNP-138.

Yingst, Robert A. "The Taking of Via Mountain." 1997. Accessed January 18, 2014, http://home.comcast.net/~jvia/viamtn.htm.

Zerkel, L. Ferdinand, to Hon. Wm. E. Carson, Chairman. December 11, 1933. RMR 21206, box 99, folder 7.

———, to Mr. E. D. Freeland, Supt. April 7, 1947. SCCD 21203, box 49, folder 14.